Betty Crocker's

COOKING FOR ONE

GOLDEN PRESS/NEW YORK

Western Publishing Company, Inc.
Racine, Wisconsin

Director of Photography: George Ancona
Illustrator: Roland Rodegast

First Printing This Edition, 1984

Printed in U.S.A. by Western Publishing Company, Inc.
Published by Golden Press, New York, New York.
Library of Congress Catalog Card Number: 83-82224

Golden® and Golden Press® are trademarks of Western Publishing Company, Inc.
ISBN 0-307-09944-X

Contents

Foreword

Alone in the kitchen? It may sound like a paradox, but you have a lot of company. A large and ever-growing number live the single life these days. This book, then, is for all of you: the person "soloing" for the first time . . . the experienced "one" looking for fresh mealtime ideas . . . the "returnee" single out of practice in dealing with scaled-down meals. You all have one thing in common: freedom of choice. And that's what *Betty Crocker's Cooking for One* is all about.

You'll find complete menus, single-serving recipes and basic information geared to the household of one. "When You're Coping with Cooking for One" has suggestions for planning and organizing. "When There's No Time to Spare" offers satisfying ways to beat the clock and "When the Budget's in a Bind" helps with ideas for how you can pinch pennies without feeling deprived. "When Your Freezer Comes to the Rescue" helps you take advantage of time when you have it so you can put away for the future, while "When the Day Calls For Something Special" could inspire you to treat yourself like company. Finally, "When One Meal Leads to Another" presents a creative approach for turning leftovers into planned-overs.

Most of the recipes in this book will probably be served for the main meal of the day, but who's to say when that will be? As the only person you need to please, you might well decide on Chicken Livers in Toast Cup as a hearty breakfast or a festive Mushroom and Alfalfa Omelet for lunch.

We hope that these menus and recipes, developed and tested in the Betty Crocker Kitchens, will help to make cooking for one singularly rewarding.

Betty Crocker

When You're Coping With Cooking For One

"Planning...shopping... storing...there's so much to do even before I cook. Is it worth it for just one?"

Effort? Yes. But worth it? Definitely. Who's more important than you? Call it challenge coupled with just rewards. Mostly, the challenges involve organization and planning. Since the kitchen sized for one may well mean minimal space, you should first decide what equipment and staples are "musts." The next step is planning nutritious and varied meals within time and money limits. Then, you'll need to find out how to survive in a world geared to the "giant economy size."

Here, then, is a Master Plan for meeting the challenges of cooking for one. Rewards? They can be summed up in one word: freedom—freedom to plan the meals you want and freedom to enjoy them when and where you want.

ORGANIZING THE KITCHEN

Organization is the key to cooking without panic. Even if it takes more time than you think you care to give it, put your kitchen and food supplies in order, and you will have half the battle won. The well-organized cook, working in the well-organized kitchen, will know that all ingredients for a particular recipe are on hand...that the pot is the right size for the stew...and that the freezer, refrigerator and cupboards can come to the rescue in an emergency.

Start by taking stock of your "tools." The chart at right lists the basics. With these, you will be able to prepare a wide variety of recipes, including all of those in this book. In addition, you may want to consider the optional equipment to give you an "extra hand." Finally, you have a choice of special appliances—from blenders and toaster-ovens to food processors and microwaves—to brighten and broaden your cooking efforts. And, though you may consider a microwave a substantial investment, especially for one, it will certainly save time, energy and messy cleanup chores. Plus the microwave is most efficient when small quantities of food are being prepared.

Next, tableware—how much you need depends on the type and amount of entertaining you do, but figure on having at least enough to serve four. You should have dinner plates, dessert and/or salad plates, soup and/or cereal bowls, cups and saucers and/or mugs. In addition, it's nice to have small dessert dishes and individual salad bowls. However, don't feel that you have to have the traditional "service for four." The necessity for the "perfect match" has given way to the fun and flexibility of mix-and-match and even one-of-a-kind.

Your flatware will include the usual fork, knife and teaspoon and, if possible, salad or dessert forks, soup spoons, steak knives and serving pieces. The all-purpose 10-ounce stemmed goblet is a great way to solve the glassware problem if you're strapped for space or money. If not, you can add regular water tumblers, juice, wine and iced-tea glasses.

Every Kitchen for One Needs

For Preparation	For Cooking
Set of nested dry measuring cups	Custard cups (6-ounce)
Liquid measuring cups (1-cup, 1-quart)	Casseroles (20-ounce, 1-quart)
Measuring spoons	Covered skillets (6-inch, 8-inch, 10-inch)
Set of mixing bowls	Covered saucepans (1-quart, 2-quart, 3-quart)
Wooden spoons	
Rubber scrapers (wide and narrow)	Small roasting pan (with rack)
Acrylic cutting board	Baking pan (8x8x2 or 9x9x2 inches)
French knife	
Paring knife	Cookie sheet
Utility knife (long, narrow-handled)	Muffin pan
Frozen food knife	Pie plates (6-inch, 9-inch)
Utility fork (long-tined, long-handled)	Wire cooling rack
Pancake turner	Pot holders
Slotted spoon	
Ladle	**For Added Convenience**
Wire whip	
Tongs	Cheese cutter
Kitchen scissors	Melon ball cutter
Can opener	Individual gelatin molds
Bottle and jar opener	Omelet pan
Grater (4-sided combined grater and shredder)	Jelly roll pan (15½x10½x1 inch)
Strainer	Individual loaf pans (4½x2½x1½ inches)
Hand beater	Pie pan (4¼x1¼ inches)
Rolling pin	Teakettle
Kitchen timer	Coffee maker

Table linens? No problem. For the most part, you'll probably use place mats with matching or contrasting napkins in both paper and easy-care fabrics. If you do have a special tablecloth, keep it handy for times when you're in the mood to treat yourself like a guest.

As for table accessories, keep your eyes open for interesting pieces at flea markets, garage sales and special store events. A one-of-a-kind Victorian teacup may be priced just right. And you'll enjoy the thrill of discovery and set an original-looking table in the bargain.

If your particular situation requires cutting back, not adding to, then weed out! Keep what you're sure you'll use and store, sell or give away the rest. In either case, the message is "feel free"; depart from the ordinary. Serve soup in a mug, pudding in a wine glass, jam in an egg cup. Forget the traditional floral arrangement and treat your table to a picture-perfect basket of fruit, a collection of candles, an exotic fresh flower or two. In short, you're free to do the unexpected.

STOCKING THE SHELVES

Although you will be preparing meals with your own preferences in mind, every well-stocked cupboard, refrigerator and freezer should have most of the following standard items on hand.

Staples

Buttermilk baking mix	Relishes
Cornstarch	Jams, jellies and honey
Sugars (granulated, brown, powdered)	Coffee and tea
Baking powder	Special herbs and spices
Baking soda	Grated Parmesan cheese
Vanilla	Coconut
Salt and pepper	Breakfast cereals
Seasoned salt	Instant soup, sauce and gravy mixes
Vegetable shortening	Single-serving canned soups (7½-ounce size)
Vinegar	
Worcestershire sauce	
Red pepper sauce	
Rice	Single-serving canned fruits and vegetables (8-ounce size)
Spaghetti, macaroni and noodles	
Salad dressings	Frozen main dishes, potatoes, vegetables, fruits, desserts and fruit juices
Instant beef and chicken bouillon	
Instant minced onion or onion powder	
Instant minced garlic or garlic powder	
Parsley flakes	
Mustard and catsup	
Pickles and olives	

PLANNING MEALS

The menus in this book were designed to help you plan a variety of nutritionally balanced meals that fit a variety of needs. But don't feel you must be bound by them. Use the chart below and the information on the pages that follow as a guide to understanding the basics of good nutrition; then make the right choices to satisfy your taste, mood and budget.

A Daily Food Guide

Fruits and Vegetables
4 Servings Daily
Include one Vitamin C source (oranges, grapefruit) each day and one Vitamin A source (spinach, carrots) every other day.

1 serving =
½ cup or typical portion (1 medium potato, 1 orange, ½ grapefruit, 1 cup raw leafy vegetables)

Breads and Cereals
4 Servings Daily
Select whole grain, enriched, restored or fortified products.

1 serving =
1 slice bread, ½ to ¾ cup cooked cereal, cornmeal, pasta, grits or 1 cup ready-to-eat cereal

Milk and Cheese
2 Servings Daily

1 serving =
1 cup milk, ⅔ cup yogurt, 1½ cups ice cream, two 1-inch cubes Cheddar or Swiss cheese or 1½ cups cream soup

Meat, Poultry, Fish and Beans
2 Servings Daily

1 serving =
2 to 3 ounces lean cooked meat, poultry or fish, 2 eggs, 1 cup cooked dried beans or peas, 4 tablespoons peanut butter or other nut butters, ½ cup seeds, 1 to 1½ cups nuts

Fats, Sweets and Alcohol
Number and amount of servings vary according to caloric needs.

For example, try a peanut butter and jelly sandwich or a thin cubed steak on toast for breakfast. Add some fruit and a glass of milk and you have a refreshing change-of-pace start for the day. Or, if the menu suggestion is broccoli and you prefer something different, ½ cup of a cooked vegetable or 1 cup of salad can be served instead. What you eat is up to you. But to ensure a well-balanced diet, be sure to meet your daily food requirements.

To survive and thrive, you need a variety of foods, each with its own special nutrients—the chemical substances that help growth, repair tissues, furnish energy and regulate body processes. As you will see from the list that follows, nutrients are grouped as proteins, carbohydrates and fats and vitamins, minerals and water.

Nutrients in Foods

Proteins: It is wise to combine complete proteins from meats, eggs and cheese with incomplete proteins from breads, cereals, dried beans and peas.

Carbohydrates: Major sources of carbohydrates are whole grain foods, fruits and vegetables. Nutritionists are encouraging increased consumption of these carbohydrates in everyday diets. Starches (pasta and bread) and sugars also supply carbohydrates.

Fats: Fat is a nutrient found in many foods. Fatty meats, most cheeses and nuts are some important sources.

Vitamins: Citrus fruits are a major source of vitamin C; liver, deep yellow and dark green vegetables, whole and enriched grains, milk and eggs are excellent sources of other essential vitamins.

Minerals: Good sources are seafood, milk and milk products, whole and enriched grains and eggs.

Water: Remember, water is second only to oxygen as being essential to life! You should drink six or more cups of liquid (including juices and broth) each day to provide some of the water your body needs. Fruits, vegetables and milk also supply water.

Fiber

The fiber content in food also plays an important and beneficial role in the diet. Fiber is derived mainly from whole grain cereals and breads, fruits and vegetables and nuts. For example, bran cereals, whole wheat breads and other foods made from whole wheat grains, such as whole ground cornmeal, whole rolled oats and brown rice, retain the outer coat of the cereal grain which contains the most fiber. Fruits and vegetables contain fiber, although in variable amounts, as do roasted nuts, sesame seed, sunflower seeds and nuts, and coconut.

Nonmeat Protein Food

Finally, with the great interest in vegetarian foods and rising food prices, take a look at the value of nonmeat foods. For adults, daily meals and snacks should total about 65 grams protein.

Nonmeat Protein Foods

	Amount	Protein Grams
Milk (all kinds)	1 cup	9
Cottage cheese	¼ cup	8
Cheese		
Cheddar	1 ounce	7
Swiss	1 ounce	8
Egg	1	6
Yogurt	½ cup	4
Peanut butter	2 tablespoons	8
Imitation bacon	2 tablespoons	8
Soybeans	½ cup cooked	8
Lentils	½ cup cooked	8
Peas, dried	½ cup cooked	8
Flour	½ cup	7
Oatmeal	1 cup cooked	5
Cornmeal	1 cup cooked	3
Bread		
brown	1 slice	3
white	1 slice	2
Noodles	½ cup cooked	3
Rice	½ cup cooked	2

For comparison, there are 17 grams protein in a 3-ounce cooked hamburger, 18 grams protein in a 3-ounce chicken drumstick, 25 grams protein in 1 thick pork chop (3.5 ounces), 5 grams protein in 1 breaded fish stick and 16 grams protein in 3 ounces canned tuna.

SHOPPING

The challenge of shopping begins even before you step into a store. It starts with the need for a menu plan—preferably for a week's worth of the meals you know you'll be preparing at home. This ensures the best use of the foods you buy and leaves a minimum of waste.

A list is imperative. Keep it where you can conveniently jot down your needs as you think of them or as you run short. Have your list handy, too, when you read the newspaper on "food day," so you can note the specials and possibly plan around them. And most important, keep that list firmly in hand while you shop—as your own personal defense against excessive impulse buying.

Try to pick up the majority of the items on your list in one trip. An exception, of course, will be perishables or foods such as fresh fish, which are best prepared the same day, if possible.

It's also wise to shop during nonrush hours. Though it's probably easiest to shop on the way home from work, that's when the stores are most crowded and you're probably hungry. Hungry people are likely to do more impulse buying than those who have eaten. Consider treating yourself to a meal out on shopping day and shop after the rush hours.

Resist the temptation to buy that package of six glorious tomatoes that's a steal. What price bargain when you can neither store nor consume it? The deli sections of supermarkets are good places to find just-for-one buys. But since more and more markets are recognizing the existence of the one-member household, look for smaller quantities to start showing up in all departments. And when you hear about an unbeatable "special," why not plan to entertain or make an arrangement with a friend or neighbor and share the wealth?

If canned goods are on your list, the 8-ounce-size cans are definitely for you. They may cost more, but you'll eliminate a lot of unwanted leftovers. If you have shelf space, buy more than one if that price is better. The freezer section also offers a large selection of single-serving main dishes, side dishes and multi-course dinners. And you'll find a variety of choices—from low-calorie dishes to gourmet meals.

Fruits and vegetables can vary greatly in price and quality from season to season. Be sure to buy only very fresh, undamaged produce and avoid foods that are overripe or possibly deteriorated. Use the following charts (below and on page 10) to help you buy wisely and in season.

Seasonal Buying Guide

Vegetables	Peak Season
Artichokes	October to June
Asparagus	March to July
Beans	May to November
Beets	June to November
Broccoli	October to May
Brussels sprouts	September to March
Cabbage	All year
Carrots	All year
Cauliflower	September to May
Celery	All year
Chinese cabbage	All year
Corn, sweet	May to October
Cucumbers	All year
Eggplant	All year
Endive and escarole	All year
Garlic	All year
Lettuce and other greens	All year
Mushrooms	All year
Okra	May to October
Onions	All year
Parsley and herbs	All year
Parsnips	All year
Peas	February to September
Peppers	All year
Potatoes	All year
Pumpkins	September and October
Radishes	All year
Spinach	January to July
Sweet potatoes and squash	All year
Tomatoes	All year
Turnips and rutabagas	September to April

When buying fruit, look for the best eating quality rather than appearance. "Good looks" does not always mean good quality. Though many fruits are in season throughout the year, they are less costly during peak seasons.

Seasonal Buying Guide

Fruit	Peak Season
Apples	September to April
Apricots	June and July
Avocados	All year
Bananas	All year
Blueberries	June to August
Cantaloupe	May to October
Cherries, sweet	June to August
Cranberries	September to February
Grapefruit	October to June
Grapes	June to January
Kiwi fruit	June to March
Lemons and limes	All year
Melons, honeydew	March to November
Nectarines	June to October
Oranges	November to July
Peaches	June to October
Pears, Bartlett	July to December
D'Anjou	October to June
Pineapple	April to June
Plums	June to October
Pomegranates	September to January
Raspberries	June to August
Rhubarb	January to August
Strawberries	May to July
Tangerines	November to March
Watermelon	May to September

Finally, it helps to know how much you'll get from what you've bought. Use the Kitchen Math chart on page 11 for guidance.

STORING

You can probably make do with containers acquired free: coffee cans, glass jars, single-serving freezer trays and pans. When they've served their original purpose, wash and use them for your own needs.

Shelf Storage

Proper shelf storage means using airtight containers and keeping them away from light and heat. Store cereals, pasta, rice and dry bread crumbs in tightly closed containers in a cool, dry place away from soaps or foods with strong odors.

Store all canned foods (except those requiring refrigeration) in a cool, dry place with good air space around them. Properly stored canned foods will keep almost indefinitely, but it is wise to rotate your stock and use the older ones first.

Ultra heat treated milk is aseptically packaged for shelf storage. Unopened, it can be stored up to six months. Nonfat dry milk can be stored in a cool place for several months, while dry whole milk, which contains fat, should be refrigerated and used within a few weeks.

Refrigerator Storage

Be sure the refrigerator is set at 40° or lower. Foods stored in the refrigerator should be covered, wrapped or bagged. Reserve the coldest part of the refrigerator for poultry, fish and dairy products. Meats, poultry and fish can be refrigerated for 1 to 2 days. Fresh milk products should be stored in the refrigerator in covered containers and used within 5 days.

Freezer Storage

Freezer storage demands a temperature of 0° or lower. Invest in a freezer thermometer and check it frequently to be sure your freezer is actually maintaining the proper temperature.

The faster your food freezes, the better it retains flavor and texture. Food packages should be in direct contact with the freezing surface, and at least 1 inch apart so the air can circulate. Once the food is frozen solid, you can stack the packages.

In addition to labeling each freezer package, keep a current record of the contents of your freezer, including the date the food was frozen and the date by which it should be used. Remember to consult this record when planning meals and making shopping lists. (For additional freezer tips, see pages 41-58.)

Food	If you have...	You'll get...
Apple	1 medium	1 cup chopped
Banana	1 to 2 medium	1 cup sliced
	3 medium	1 cup mashed
Beans, dried (small)	8 ounces	3 cups cooked
Butter or margarine	1 pound	2 cups
	¼ pound or 1 stick	½ cup
Cabbage	¼ pound	1 cup shredded
Carrots	1 to 2 medium	1 cup shredded
	2 to 3 medium	1 cup thinly sliced
Celery	2 medium stalks	1 cup sliced
Cheese		
Cheddar or American	4 ounces	1 cup shredded
cottage	8 ounces	1 cup
cream	3-ounce package	6 tablespoons
	8-ounce package	1 cup (16 tablespoons)
Chicken (cooked)	2½-pound broiler-fryer	2 cups diced
Chocolate		
chips	6-ounce package	1 cup
unsweetened	8-ounce package	8 squares (1 ounce each)
Cereal (flakes)	3 cups	1 cup crushed
Crackers		
graham	12 squares	1 cup fine crumbs
soda	20 squares	1 cup coarse crumbs
Cream		
sour	8 ounces	1 cup
whipping	1 cup (½ pint)	2 cups whipped
Flour		
all-purpose	1 pound	3½ cups
cake	1 pound	4 cups
Green pepper	1 medium	1 cup chopped
Lemon		
juice	1 medium	2 to 3 tablespoons
peel	1 medium	1½ teaspoons grated
Macaroni (elbow)	½ of 8-ounce package	2 cups cooked
Meat (cooked)	6 to 7 ounces	1 cup julienne strips
Milk (evaporated)	1 can (6 ounces)	⅔ cup
	1 can (14½ ounces)	1⅔ cups
Noodles (regular)	4 ounces	2 cups cooked
Nuts	4 ounces (shelled)	1 cup chopped
Onions	1 medium	½ cup chopped
Rice		
brown	½ cup (uncooked)	1¾ to 2 cups cooked
parboiled (converted)	½ cup (uncooked)	1½ to 1¾ cups cooked
precooked (instant)	1 cup (uncooked)	1 to 2 cups cooked
regular white	½ cup (uncooked)	1½ cups cooked
wild	½ cup (uncooked)	1½ cups cooked
Strawberries	1 pint	2 cups sliced
Sugar		
brown (firmly packed)	1 pound	2¼ cups
confectioners' (unsifted)	1 pound	4 cups
granulated	1 pound	2¼ cups

KEEPING FOOD SAFE

It is important to keep cooked food either hot or cold. Don't allow hot or cold foods to remain at room temperature for more than 2 hours; bacteria thrive in lukewarm food. These germs seldom change the taste, odor or appearance of the food, so you have no way of knowing how safe the food is unless you follow this rule: Hot foods should be kept hot (above 140°) and cold foods cold (40°).

Keep cooked food hot until serving time or refrigerate as soon as possible. If it will not raise the refrigerator temperature above 45°, hot food can be placed in the refrigerator immediately. Refrigerate leftovers as soon as possible.

To keep food safe, it, you and the environment must be kept clean. The best place to start is with your hands. Germs are a natural part of the environment and if you keep germs off meat, poultry and dairy products, you'll avoid problems. Keep utensils, platters and countertops soap-and-hot-water clean. Don't handle food if you have infected cuts or sores on your hands.

Be careful not to transfer germs from raw meat to cooked meat. Do not, for example, carry raw hamburgers to the range on a platter then later serve the cooked meat on the same (unwashed) platter. Another danger spot for food is the wooden chopping board. An acrylic cutting board is less porous and far safer to use. Wash cutting boards with a mixture of 2 teaspoons chlorine bleach and 1 teaspoon vinegar to a gallon of water.

And, though many singles view their pets as good friends, this is one friend that does not belong in the kitchen when you're preparing food.

Certain foods require more safety considerations than others:

Ground Meat: Cook thoroughly since it's handled often in preparation and germs can get mixed into it. Never, never, eat raw ground meat—it's not safe!

Ham: Know what kind of ham you're buying; some are fully cooked, others need cooking. Check the label. If you have any doubts, cook it.

Frankfurters, Luncheon Meat: Refrigerate; use within a week. Use a fork or tongs when you handle the meat. Freeze frankfurters up to 2 weeks. Do not freeze luncheon meat.

Poultry: Cook all poultry products as long as directions require. Refrigerate cooked poultry, stuffing and giblets as soon as possible in separate containers. Use within a few days or freeze.

Canned Foods: Do not buy or use food from leaking, bulging or dented cans or from jars with cracked or loose or bulging lids. If you're in doubt about a food, don't taste it. Return it to your grocer and report it to your local health authority.

ENJOYING THE REWARDS

Let's assume that the challenges of organizing the kitchen, planning mealtime strategy, managing the shopping and storing have all been met. It's time now to enjoy the promised rewards of singleness: freedom. You're free to eat *when* you choose—no need to delay the meal for a latecomer. You're free to eat *where* you choose—no reason to be tied to the same spot night after night. You're free to eat *what* you choose. Think of it! All the options are yours. So make up your mind to make the most of them and you'll get the most out of "cooking for one."

When There's No Time To Spare

"When I'm in a hurry, I just grab whatever's handy and eat it on the run. There really ought to be a better way."

Well, there is. With a few "ready reserves" in your freezer, refrigerator and cupboard to rescue you from last-minute panic, there's no need to resort to a catch-as-catch-can meal. The 14 menus on the following pages show you just how easy it can be. For example, start with ¼ pound of ground beef. In little more time than it takes to cook a hamburger, you can put together a Mexican-inspired main-dish salad, or a beef and zucchini casserole — each with speedy go-withs.

Imagination and planning go hand in hand in all of these minute-minded meals. And for super speed, microwave directions have been included with many of the recipes.

MUSTARD POTATO FRANKS
WALDORF SALAD
RYE TOAST
CHOCOLATE BRÛLÉE

Mustard Potato Franks

Mustard Potatoes (below)
2 frankfurters or smoked sausage links
1 tablespoon shredded cheese

Prepare Mustard Potatoes. Split frankfurters lengthwise, not cutting completely through. Flatten frankfurters; place cut sides up on rack in broiler pan or on ungreased cookie sheet. Spread frankfurters with Mustard Potatoes; sprinkle with cheese.

Set oven control to broil and/or 550°. Broil frankfurters with tops about 5 inches from heat until cheese is melted, 4 to 5 minutes.

MUSTARD POTATOES

⅓ cup water
1 tablespoon milk
1 teaspoon margarine or butter
⅛ teaspoon salt
⅓ cup mashed potato mix (dry)
1 teaspoon parsley flakes
½ teaspoon prepared mustard

Heat water, milk, margarine and salt to boiling in 1-quart saucepan. Remove from heat; stir in remaining ingredients with fork until desired consistency.

To Microwave: Microwave water, milk, margarine and salt uncovered in 1-pint microwaveproof measure to boiling on high (full) power, about 2 minutes. Stir in remaining ingredients. Place split frankfurters, cut sides up, on microwaveproof plate. Spread with Mustard Potatoes; sprinkle with cheese. Microwave uncovered on high (full) power until cheese is melted and frankfurters are hot, 1 to 2 minutes.

Waldorf Salad

½ medium apple, coarsely chopped
1 small stalk celery, sliced
2 tablespoons salted peanuts
2 tablespoons mayonnaise or salad dressing
Lettuce cup

Mix apple, celery, peanuts and mayonnaise; spoon into lettuce cup.

Chocolate Brûlée

½ cup prepared chocolate pudding
1 tablespoon packed brown sugar
1 tablespoon flaked coconut
1 teaspoon margarine or butter, softened

Spoon pudding into 6-ounce custard cup. Mix remaining ingredients; spoon onto pudding. Set oven control to broil and/or 550°. Broil pudding with top about 5 inches from heat until coconut is golden brown and topping is bubbly, about 4 minutes.

Should Know...

The microwave is a big plus for the single-person household—it saves cooking time, clean-up time and energy (your own and the local utility's). Since more and more people are microwaving, we've added microwave directions to some of the recipes in this book. These recipes were tested using high (full) power settings (unless otherwise indicated), and you will achieve best results by using the same settings. Also note that in these recipes, "cover" means that no steam or moisture should escape. The container should be covered with a fitted lid or sealed with vented plastic wrap. "Cover loosely" requires only a waxed-paper covering or a lid slightly ajar.

Ham-Banana Salad

½ cup ½-inch cubes fully cooked
    smoked ham
1 medium stalk celery, sliced
2 green onions (with tops), sliced
1 small banana, cut into ¼-inch slices
2 tablespoons bottled sweet-and-sour
    dressing
    Salad greens

Toss ham, celery, onions, banana and dressing. Serve on salad greens.

Oniony Muffin

Toast 1 split English muffin. Spread each half with margarine or butter; sprinkle with onion salt.

Orange Cooler

⅓ cup milk
2 scoops orange sherbet
    Sparkling water or ginger ale

Mix milk and 1 scoop orange sherbet in tall glass until smooth. Add 1 scoop orange sherbet; fill glass with sparkling water. Garnish with orange slice if desired. Serve immediately.

Ham and Turkey Sandwich

1 hamburger bun or hard roll, split
    Bottled blue cheese dressing
5 thin slices smoked ham (about 1 ounce)
1 slice process American cheese
    (¾ ounce)
4 thin slices smoked turkey (about
    1 ounce)

Spread each half bun with dressing. Place ham on bottom half of bun; top with cheese and turkey. Cover with top half of bun. Wrap sandwich in aluminum foil. Heat in 425° oven until meat is hot and cheese is melted, 15 to 20 minutes.

Artichoke Salad

1 cup bite-size pieces salad greens
1 jar (6 ounces) marinated artichoke
    hearts, chilled and drained (reserve
    1 to 2 tablespoons marinade)
6 pitted ripe olives, cut into halves
4 tomato wedges

Toss salad greens, artichoke hearts, olives and tomato wedges; drizzle with reserved marinade.

Brandied Caramel Apple

1 teaspoon brandy
2 tablespoons caramel topping
1 medium apple, sliced
    Sliced almonds

Drizzle brandy and caramel topping over apple slices. Sprinkle with almonds.

**SCALLOPED POTATOES
AND HAM
BUTTERED BROCCOLI
BREADSTICKS
HONEY-WINE PEACHES**

Scalloped Potatoes and Ham

⅓ package (5.25-ounce size) scalloped
    potato mix
¾ cup boiling water
⅓ cup ½-inch cubes fully cooked smoked
    ham
¼ cup milk
2 teaspoons margarine or butter

Measure contents of 1 package scalloped
potatoes; divide into thirds (about ⅔ cup
potato slices and 1 tablespoon plus 2 teaspoons Sauce Mix). Mix all ingredients in
ungreased 1-quart casserole. Cook uncovered in 400° oven until potatoes are tender,
25 to 30 minutes.

Note: To store remaining mix, place potato
slices and Sauce Mix in small plastic storage bags. Secure bags tightly and store in
closed package. Use within 2 weeks. Omit
ham if desired and follow directions above.

To Microwave: Mix all ingredients in ungreased 1-quart microwaveproof casserole
or bowl. Cover tightly and microwave on
high (full) power until potatoes are tender,
11 to 12 minutes.

Honey-Wine Peaches

1 tablespoon honey
1 tablespoon dry white wine
1 peach, sliced, or 1 can (8 ounces) sliced
    peaches, drained

Mix honey and wine. Spoon over peach
slices.

**QUICK CHEESE BROIL
AVOCADO-TOMATO SALAD
FRESH FRUIT SLUSH**

Quick Cheese Broil

2 slices (¾ inch thick) French bread,
    toasted, or 1 hard roll, split and
    toasted
2 tablespoons beer or dry white wine
2 slices (7x4 inches each) Swiss cheese,
    cut into halves
Seasoned salt

Place toast in individual casserole or on
double thickness aluminum foil. Drizzle
beer over each slice toast; top with cheese.
Set oven control to broil and/or 550°. Broil
toast with tops about 5 inches from heat
until cheese is melted and bubbly, about 2
minutes; sprinkle with seasoned salt. Garnish with mustard sprouts if desired.

Avocado-Tomato Salad

1 small avocado, cut into ¼-inch slices
1 small tomato, cut into wedges
    Lettuce leaf
    Bottled Italian dressing

Arrange avocado slices and tomato wedges
on lettuce leaf; drizzle with dressing.

Fresh Fruit Slush

1 cup vanilla ice cream
½ teaspoon lemon juice
½ cup strawberries, raspberries, cubed
    pineapple, sliced peaches or sliced
    bananas

Blend all ingredients in blender or small
mixer bowl just until smooth. Serve with
cocktail straw and dessert spoon.

QUICK RAREBIT
GREEN BEANS
ORANGE-APPLE SALAD
CHOCOLATE BROWNIE

Quick Rarebit

½ jar (5-ounce size) pasteurized
    Neufchâtel cheese spread with
    olive and pimiento (¼ cup)
½ jar (2½-ounce size) sliced mushrooms
    (about 2 tablespoons drained)
1 green onion (with top), sliced
1 tablespoon milk
2 drops red pepper sauce
2 tomato slices
1 English muffin, split and toasted

Heat cheese spread, mushrooms, onion, milk and pepper sauce over medium heat, stirring occasionally, until hot and bubbly, about 2 minutes. Place tomato slice on each muffin half. Pour cheese sauce over each tomato slice. Garnish with snipped parsley if desired.

To Microwave: Mix cheese spread, mushrooms, onion, milk and pepper sauce in 1-pint microwaveproof measure. Microwave uncovered on high (full) power 1 minute; stir. Microwave uncovered on high (full) power until hot and bubbly, about 1 minute.

Orange-Apple Salad

1 small orange, pared and sectioned
½ medium apple, cut into wedges
    Lettuce leaf
    Bottled French dressing
    Celery seed

Arrange orange sections and apple slices on lettuce leaf; drizzle with dressing. Sprinkle with celery seed.

CHEESY CORN CHOWDER
SPINACH-CAULIFLOWER SALAD
SESAME CRACKERS
MINTY LEMON SHERBET

Cheesy Corn Chowder

2 slices bacon, cut into ½-inch pieces
2 tablespoons chopped onion
1 tablespoon chopped celery
1 can (8½ ounces) cream-style corn
⅓ cup milk
½ teaspoon seasoned salt
 Dash of pepper
2 tablespoons shredded cheese
 Snipped parsley

Fry bacon in 1½-quart saucepan until crisp; remove bacon and drain. Remove all but 1 tablespoon bacon fat from saucepan. Stir onion and celery into fat in saucepan. Cook and stir until onion is tender. Stir in corn, milk, seasoned salt and pepper. Heat to boiling, stirring occasionally. Remove from heat; stir in bacon. Pour into bowl; sprinkle with cheese and parsley.

To Microwave: Place bacon in ungreased 1-quart microwaveproof casserole; cover loosely. Microwave on high (full) power until crisp, 2 to 3 minutes; remove bacon and drain. Remove all but 1 tablespoon bacon fat from casserole. Stir onion and celery into fat in casserole. Cover tightly and microwave on high (full) power until onion is tender, about 3 minutes. Stir in corn, milk, seasoned salt and pepper. Cover tightly and microwave on high (full) power until hot and bubbly around edge, 2 to 2½ minutes; stir in bacon. Sprinkle with cheese and parsley.

Spinach-Cauliflower Salad

½ can (11-ounce size) mandarin orange
 segments (about ½ cup drained)
½ cup bite-size pieces spinach
¼ cup cauliflowerets
1 tablespoon bottled French dressing

Toss all ingredients.

Minty Lemon Sherbet

1 teaspoon crème de menthe or crème de
 menthe syrup
1 scoop lemon sherbet
 Coconut

Drizzle crème de menthe over sherbet. Sprinkle with coconut.

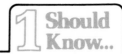

Should Know...

Cheese is handy to have on hand—as an ingredient as well as a snack. If tightly wrapped after opening, soft cheeses will keep in the refrigerator up to 2 weeks; hard cheeses will keep several months. Grating and shredding are good do-it-yourself ways to use up odds and ends of cheese. Any cheese that has become dry and hard can be grated, while moist cheese can be shredded.

Taco Salad

¼ pound ground beef
2 tablespoons chili sauce
¼ teaspoon chili powder
¼ teaspoon salt
2 to 4 drops red pepper sauce
2 cups bite-size pieces salad greens
1 small tomato, cut into wedges
1 small avocado, thinly sliced
1 tablespoon chopped onion
   Chili Dressing (below)
1 package (¾ ounce) corn chips (about
   ½ cup)

Cook and stir ground beef until brown; drain. Stir in chili sauce, chili powder, salt and pepper sauce; cool 5 minutes. Toss salad greens, tomato, avocado and onion in large bowl. Add beef mixture and Chili Dressing; toss. Sprinkle with corn chips.

CHILI DRESSING

Mix 2 tablespoons mayonnaise or salad dressing and 1 tablespoon chili sauce.

Limeade

1 cup water
⅓ cup lime juice (about 3 limes)
¼ cup sugar

Mix all ingredients. Serve over ice. 2 servings (¾ cup each).

Zesty Beef Bake

¼ pound ground beef
1 small zucchini, cut into ¼-inch slices
1 small onion, thinly sliced
½ teaspoon salt
¼ teaspoon pepper
   Zesty Sauce (below)

Cook and stir ground beef, zucchini, onion, salt and pepper over medium heat until beef is brown; drain. Spoon beef mixture into individual casserole or pie plate, 6x1 inch. Spread Zesty Sauce over beef mixture. Cook uncovered in 450° oven until sauce is bubbly and golden brown, 10 to 12 minutes.

ZESTY SAUCE

2 tablespoons dairy sour cream
2 tablespoons mayonnaise or salad
   dressing
1 teaspoon prepared mustard
⅛ teaspoon chili powder
   Dash of ground cinnamon

Mix all ingredients.

Grape Toss

1 tablespoon bottled French dressing
1 teaspoon lemon juice
1 cup bite-size pieces salad greens
½ cup Tokay or green grape halves,
   seeded
   Coconut

Mix dressing and lemon juice; toss with salad greens and grapes. Sprinkle with coconut.

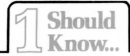

About Salad Greens and Special Dressings

A tossed green salad is the perfect hurry-up "fresh" vegetable. Just keep in mind a few basics:

Know Your Greens: Four main groups of the many varieties of lettuce are commonly available. Crisphead (iceberg); butterhead (Boston and Bibb), with its tender leaves; romaine (also called cos), with crisp, elongated dark leaves; and leaf lettuce, red or green with tender leaves that don't form heads. The endive family includes curly endive, escarole and Belgian and French endive (blanched, narrow leaves that grow in compact upright clusters). And don't forget "variety" greens such as watercress, spinach, mustard greens, celery leaves, beet tops, Chinese cabbage, even dandelion and nasturtium leaves. Vary the light with the dark, the tender with the crisp.

Handle with Care: Store your greens in the refrigerator in a covered container or plastic bag. Watercress, parsley and fresh herbs, however, should be stored tightly covered. Wash greens only as you need them, but several hours before using (they need time to crisp). Tear, don't cut, salad greens into bite-size pieces, unless the recipe calls for an iceberg slice or wedge. Strip Belgian endives into whole leaves, or cut into slices and pull apart onion-fashion.

Add Some Pizazz: Try a sprinkling of salted nuts, croutons, French fried onions, crisply fried and crumbled bacon, crumbled blue cheese or sliced olives. For color, add carrot curls, sliced radishes, a sliced hard-cooked egg or cherry tomatoes. Team pale iceberg lettuce with dark green spinach, romaine and/ or curly endive. Bronze lettuce provides color and delicate flavor.

Personalized Salad Dressings: Take advantage of the wonderful variety of prepared salad dressings available and add an extra touch to give them the taste of homemade. Use the suggestions that follow for starters, then create your own.

Add the dressing just before serving your salad and use only enough to coat the leaves lightly. Toss gently. Store all salad dressings in tightly covered jars in the refrigerator. Shake thoroughly before using.

To 1 tablespoon oil and vinegar dressing, add a dash of chili powder.

To 1 tablespoon oil and vinegar dressing, add a sprinkle of dried oregano leaves.

To 1 tablespoon oil and vinegar dressing, add a sprinkle of dried thyme leaves.

To 1 tablespoon oil and vinegar dressing add a dash of ground savory.

To 1 tablespoon mayonnaise or salad dressing, add 1½ teaspoons catsup.

To 1 tablespoon mayonnaise or salad dressing, add 1½ teaspoons chili sauce, a dash of red pepper sauce and a dash of chili powder.

To 1 tablespoon mayonnaise or salad dressing, add 1½ teaspoons frozen whipped topping (thawed).

Dip 'n Dunk Steak Sandwich

1 beef cubed steak (about 3 ounces)
1 tablespoon vegetable oil
　Salt and pepper
⅓ cup water
½ teaspoon instant beef bouillon
¼ teaspoon seasoned salt
1 hard roll, split and toasted

Cook beef in oil over medium-high heat until brown on both sides, about 8 minutes; sprinkle with salt and pepper. Remove from skillet; keep warm. Drain fat from skillet. Pour water into skillet. Heat to boiling, scraping brown particles from bottom of skillet. Stir in instant bouillon and seasoned salt. Place beef between roll halves; cut into halves. Serve seasoned juice in small bowl. Dip sandwich into seasoned juice to eat.

Dilled Green Beans

1 can (8 ounces) cut green beans
1 teaspoon margarine or butter
⅛ teaspoon dried dill weed
　Dash of garlic salt

Heat green beans (with liquid) over medium heat until hot, about 3 minutes; drain. Stir in remaining ingredients.

Honey Strawberries

2 teaspoons honey
1 teaspoon lime juice
1 cup sliced strawberries
　Whipped topping

Mix honey and lime juice; gently stir in strawberries. Top with whipped topping.

Curried Shrimp Sandwich

¼ small cucumber, thinly sliced
1 slice raisin bread, toasted and buttered
　Salt
½ can (4¼-ounce size) medium shrimp, rinsed (about ½ cup drained)
2 tablespoons plain yogurt or dairy sour cream
1 tablespoon chopped green pepper
⅛ teaspoon curry powder
　Toasted coconut or coconut

Arrange cucumber slices on toast; sprinkle with salt. Mix shrimp, yogurt, green pepper and curry powder; spoon over cucumbers. Sprinkle with toasted coconut.

Note: Refrigerate remaining shrimp in tightly covered glass or plastic container. Store no longer than 3 days.

Mandarin Orange Sundae

Spoon ½ can (11-ounce size) mandarin orange segments (about ½ cup drained) over scoop of orange sherbet or vanilla ice cream.

11 CAN TAKE THE ROUTINE OUT OF DINNERTIME

Eggs are for breakfast. Soup and sandwiches are for lunch.
Who says? You're in charge, so try change-of-pace dinners
like these: Mushroom and Alfalfa Omelet (page 26),
Cheesy Corn Chowder (page 18), Chilled Veal and Fruit
Salad (page 85) or Curried Shrimp Sandwich (page 21).

Chicken Livers in Toast Cup

Toast Cup (below) or 1 slice white
    bread, toasted
2 ounces chicken livers, cut into 1-inch
    pieces
1 tablespoon chopped celery
1 tablespoon margarine or butter
¼ can (7½-ounce size) semi-condensed
    cream of mushroom soup
    (about ¼ cup)
    Dash of salt

Prepare Toast Cup. Cook and stir chicken
livers and celery in margarine in 1-quart
saucepan over medium heat until livers are
brown, about 5 minutes. Stir in soup and
salt. Heat until hot and bubbly, about 1 minute. Serve in Toast Cup.

TOAST CUP

Spread 1 slice white bread with margarine
or butter, softened. Press buttered side down
in ungreased 6-ounce custard cup. Toast in
375° oven until crisp and light brown, about
12 minutes.

Note: You can use remaining soup as a sauce
to serve over vegetables, omelets or open-
faced sandwiches. Heat soup until hot. Add
water or milk, if necessary, until desired
consistency.

To Microwave Chicken Livers: Microwave
1 teaspoon margarine or butter uncovered
in ungreased microwaveproof 20-ounce
casserole on medium power until melted,
about 30 seconds. Stir in chicken livers and
celery. Cover tightly and microwave on medium power until livers are brown, about 2
minutes. Stir in soup and salt. Cover tightly
and microwave on medium power until hot
and bubbly, about 1 minute.

Nutty Pea Pods

½ package (6-ounce size) frozen Chinese
    pea pods
¼ teaspoon soy sauce
    Dash of lemon pepper
1 tablespoon salted cocktail peanuts

Cook pea pods as directed on package; drain.
Toss with remaining ingredients.

Note: Use sharp knife to cut block of frozen
pea pods. Store remaining frozen pea pods
in sealed package in freezer.

Melon Sundae

1 scoop vanilla ice cream
1 chilled honeydew or cantaloupe melon
    wedge or ½ package (10-ounce size)
    frozen melon balls, partially thawed
    Strawberry or cherry topping

Place ice cream in center of melon wedge.
Drizzle with topping.

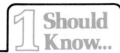

Should Know...

A fruit salad on the side, arranged on crisp
salad greens and topped with fruit dressing,
can add just the right touch of color and con-
trast to any meal. Garnished with cream
cheese balls rolled in chopped nuts or with
squares of Cheddar cheese, it can even provide a light meal. Here are some combos to
consider:
- Orange or mandarin orange segments and
apple or banana slices.
- Pear slices and Tokay grape halves.
- Pineapple spears, strawberries and blue
plum halves.
- Peach ·slices, green grapes and salted
peanuts.
- Cantaloupe pieces, dark sweet cherries and
green grapes.

Oven-fried Fish and Potatoes

- 1 frozen batter-fried fish portion
    (about 3 ounces)
- ½ jar (2½-ounce size) sliced mushrooms
    (about 2 tablespoons drained)
- 1 green onion (with top), sliced
- 1 teaspoon sliced almonds
- ½ teaspoon vegetable oil
- ½ package (14-ounce size) frozen sliced
    cottage fried potatoes (about 1 cup)
    Seasoned salt

Place fish portion in center of ungreased baking pan, 8x8x2 inches. Mix mushrooms, onion, almonds and oil; spoon over fish. Arrange potato slices in single layer around fish. Sprinkle potatoes with seasoned salt.

Cook uncovered in 450° oven until potatoes are golden brown and fish flakes easily with fork, 25 to 30 minutes. Garnish with lemon wedge and parsley if desired.

Spinach-Banana Salad

- 1 cup bite-size pieces spinach
- 1 small stalk celery, sliced
- 1 small banana, cut into ¼-inch slices
- 1 tablespoon bottled oil and vinegar
    dressing

Toss all ingredients.

Ice-Cream Sundae Sandwich

- 2 tablespoons ice cream, slightly
    softened
- 2 chocolate chip cookies (about 2½ to
    3 inches in diameter)
- ½ teaspoon chocolate-flavored syrup,
    caramel topping, almond brickle
    chips, chopped peanuts or shredded
    or flaked coconut

Spread ice cream on bottom side of 1 cookie. Top with 1 or more of the toppings and the remaining cookie.

Mushroom and Alfalfa Omelet

½ cup sliced mushrooms
2 thin onion slices
1 teaspoon margarine or butter
2 eggs
1 teaspoon water
1 tablespoon margarine or butter
  Salt and pepper
¼ cup alfalfa sprouts
  Salted sunflower nuts

Cook and stir mushrooms and onion in 1 teaspoon margarine in 8- or 9-inch omelet pan or skillet over medium heat until onion is tender, about 5 minutes. Remove and keep warm. Wipe inside of pan.

Mix eggs and water. Heat 1 tablespoon margarine in same pan over medium-high heat. As margarine melts, tilt pan in all directions to coat side thoroughly. Quickly pour eggs into pan. Slide pan back and forth rapidly over heat, stirring with fork to spread eggs continuously over bottom of pan as they thicken. Let stand over heat a few seconds to lightly brown bottom of omelet; do not overcook. (Omelet will continue to cook after folding.)

Tilt pan; run fork under edge of omelet. Fold portion of omelet nearest you in half or thirds with fork. Turn omelet onto warm plate; sprinkle with salt and pepper. Spoon warm mushrooms and onion over omelet; top with alfalfa sprouts. Sprinkle with sunflower nuts.

Melon and Strawberries

2 tablespoons plain yogurt or dairy sour cream
1 teaspoon packed brown sugar
½ cup melon balls (honeydew, cantaloupe and/or watermelon)*
½ cup sliced strawberries

Mix yogurt and brown sugar; spoon over fruit.

*1 package (10 ounces) frozen melon balls, thawed and drained, can be substituted for the fresh melon balls.

When The Budget's In A Bind

"No matter how hard I try, my baked beans pocketbook won't support my beef Wellington tastes."

If these are your sentiments, this chapter will happily prove you wrong. The message here is that one can dine handsomely on a budget, even without cheaper-by-the-dozen buys.

Learn to scout out specials and seasonal "best buys." When chicken makes sense, dress it up in a foil-wrapped dinner or oven-fry it to perfection. Apples on the bough? Bake one for dessert. Look at meat on a cost-per-serving basis. (No matter how low the per-ounce price, consider how much actual *meat* you're

buying versus the bone and fat.) Stretch ground beef in a Vegetable Meat Loaf, or opt for a satisfying meatless menu featuring Fish Stew.

Menus like these are feasts — not fasts. If you use them as your guide and learn to shop strategically, you can eat "for beans" while avoiding them as a steady diet.

BROILED LUNCHEON MEAT
AND PEACH
SWISS POTATOES
LETTUCE WITH FRENCH DRESSING
LEMON COOKIE WEDGES

Broiled Luncheon Meat and Peach

½ can (7-ounce size) pork luncheon meat,
    cut into 2 slices
1 canned peach half
1 teaspoon raspberry jelly or jam

Place meat and peach half on rack in broiler pan. Set oven control to broil and/or 550°. Broil with tops about 5 inches from heat until meat is bubbly and golden brown, about 2½ minutes. Turn meat; broil until meat is golden brown and peach half is hot, about 1 minute. Spoon jelly into center of peach half; garnish with celery leaves if desired.

Swiss Potatoes

½ can (16-ounce size) whole potatoes,
    rinsed and drained
1 teaspoon margarine or butter
2 tablespoons dry bread crumbs
    Paprika
2 tablespoons shredded Swiss cheese

Cut potatoes into ¼-inch slices. Form oblong pan, 6x4x½ inch, from aluminum foil; place on rack in broiler pan. Arrange potato slices in single layer in foil pan. Set oven control to broil and/or 550°. Broil with tops about 5 inches from heat until hot, abut 2½ minutes; dot with margarine. Sprinkle with bread crumbs, paprika and cheese. Broil until crumbs are golden brown and cheese is melted, about 1 minute. Garnish with snipped parsley if desired.

Lettuce with French Dressing

2 tablespoons olive or vegetable oil
1½ teaspoons vinegar
1½ teaspoons lemon juice
    Dash of salt
    Dash of dry mustard
    Dash of paprika
    Lettuce slice or wedge

Shake all ingredients except lettuce in tightly covered container; pour over lettuce.

Lemon Cookie Wedges

¼ cup all-purpose flour
1 tablespoon powdered sugar
2 tablespoons margarine or butter,
    softened
¼ cup granulated sugar
1 egg
2 teaspoons lemon juice
½ teaspoon grated lemon peel
⅛ teaspoon baking powder
    Dash of salt

Heat oven to 350°. Mix flour, powdered sugar and margarine. Press on bottom and halfway up side of ungreased pie pan, 4¼x1¼ inches. Bake until set, about 12 minutes. Beat remaining ingredients until light and fluffy, about 3 minutes. Pour over hot crust. Bake until no indentation remains when touched lightly in center, about 18 minutes. Cool; cut into 6 wedges. Refrigerate any remaining wedges.   6 cookie wedges.

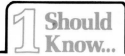

About Cooking
Various Cuts of Meat

In order to get the best value for your meat dollars, it is essential that you know how to cook various cuts of meat to the best advantage. Cooked by the wrong method, the most tender cut can become leathery; cooked by the right method, a tough cut can become tender. Know the method recommended for the cut you plan to use. There are six basic methods for cooking meat and two types of heat—dry (without liquid), used for panbroiling, panfrying, broiling and roasting, and moist (with steam or liquid), used for braising and cooking in liquid.

Although all the recipes in this book are tailored for one, cooking methods for larger cuts of meat are included here in case you're planning to entertain, want leftovers for sandwiches or salads or can take advantage of a supermarket "special" and freeze for another meal.

Panbroiling: For a tender steak or chop, sliced ham, bacon and ground meat. (All cuts should be no more than 1 inch thick.) Place meat in heavy skillet. (For very lean meat cuts, brush skillet with shortening.) Do not add fat or water; do not cover. Cook slowly; turning occasionally to brown and cook meat evenly. Pour off fat from time to time. Cook until done. Season with salt and pepper.

Panfrying: For a thin, tender steak or chop or cutlet, ground meat, liver and pieces which have been tenderized by scoring, cubing or grinding. Brown on both sides in a small amount of fat (fat is not needed in a pan with nonstick coating). Season with salt and pepper. Do not cover. Cook over medium heat, turning occasionally, until done.

Broiling: For a tender steak or chop (about ¾ inch thick), sliced ham, bacon, ground meat and baby beef liver. Broil meat surface 2 to 5 inches from heat until brown. Turn and broil to desired degree of doneness. Season with salt and pepper.

Roasting: For large, tender cuts of beef, veal, pork and lamb. Place fat side up on rack in shallow roasting pan. Insert meat thermometer so it is centered in thickest part, not resting in fat or on bone. Do not add water. Do not cover. Roast at 325° until done. For beef, 140° (rare), 160° (medium), 170° (well done). Roast all pork to 170°—except smoked ham, 160°. Lamb is done at 170-180° and veal requires 170°.

Braising: For less tender meat cuts (pot roast, round steak, short ribs) and stew meat and some tender cuts (pork chop or cutlet). Brown on all sides in heavy pan, skillet or Dutch oven, adding fat if necessary. Season with salt and pepper. Add small amount of liquid if necessary. Cover tightly. Simmer on top of range or in 300 to 325° oven until meat is tender.

Cooking in Liquid: For large, less tender meat cuts (beef corned brisket, pork hocks, lamb, beef and veal shanks) and stew meat. Brown meat on all sides in its own, or other, fat in heavy pan, skillet or Dutch oven. Cover meat with liquid. Season; cover and simmer until tender. Add vegetables just long enough before serving to cook through.

11 CAN EAT, SCRIMP AND BE MERRY

Can you feast and be frugal? Indeed you can with the hearty and filling Sausage Pocket Sandwich, shown here with Mocha Coffee (both recipes on page 31). Ingenious menus like this can go a long way toward helping you beat the budget blues.

Sausage Pocket Sandwich

Apple Slaw (below)
2 frankfurters or smoked sausage links,
    cut into ½-inch pieces*
½ medium green pepper, cut into ½-inch
    pieces
2 onion slices
1 tablespoon margarine or butter
1 pocket or pita bread

Prepare Apple Slaw; refrigerate. Cook and stir frankfurters, green pepper and onion in margarine over medium heat until onion is tender, about 10 minutes. Remove with slotted spoon. Heat pocket bread as directed on package; cut crosswise into halves. Spoon half of the Apple Slaw into each bread half. Spoon frankfurter mixture over Apple Slaw. Top with plain yogurt or dairy sour cream if desired.

*1 Polish sausage (about 5 ounces), cut lengthwise into halves, then into ½-inch pieces, can be substituted for the frankfurters.

APPLE SLAW

½ cup shredded cabbage
½ medium apple, chopped
¼ cup plain yogurt or dairy sour cream
¼ teaspoon salt
⅛ teaspoon celery seed
    Dash of pepper

Toss all ingredients.

Mocha Coffee

Fill mug ⅔ full with hot strong coffee. Top with 1 scoop (about ¼ cup) chocolate ice cream. Sprinkle with ground cinnamon.

California Coffee: Pour 2 tablespoons brandy into mug before filling with coffee.

New England Short Rib

1 tablespoon vegetable oil
1 teaspoon all-purpose flour
¼ teaspoon salt
    Dash of pepper
1 beef short rib (about 5 ounces)
1 cup water
2 teaspoons prepared horseradish
1 teaspoon instant beef bouillon
1 small rutabaga (about 8 ounces), cut
    into 3x½-inch strips
1 medium onion, cut into fourths
1 cabbage wedge (about 2 inches)

Heat oil in 8-inch skillet until hot. Mix flour, salt and pepper. Coat beef with flour mixture. Cook beef in oil over medium heat until brown; add water, horseradish and instant bouillon. Heat to boiling. Reduce heat; cover and simmer until beef is tender, about 2 hours. (Add water if necessary.)

Add rutabaga and onion; cover and simmer 15 minutes. Add cabbage; cover and simmer until tender, about 15 minutes.

Bread Pudding

1 slice bread, cut into ½-inch cubes
    (about ¾ cup)
1 egg
½ cup milk
3 tablespoons sugar
¼ teaspoon ground cinnamon
    Dash of salt

Place bread cubes in ungreased 10-ounce casserole or custard cup. Beat egg, milk, sugar, cinnamon and salt with hand beater or fork until blended. Pour egg mixture over bread cubes. Cook uncovered in 350° oven until knife inserted in center comes out clean, 40 to 45 minutes.

Oven Cheese Puff

1 slice bread, buttered and cut into
    sixths
1 egg
½ cup milk
¼ cup shredded pasteurized process
    cheese spread loaf
¼ teaspoon salt
⅛ teaspoon onion salt
6 to 8 drops red pepper sauce

Line bottom and side of ungreased 10- or 12-ounce casserole with bread pieces, buttered sides down. Beat remaining ingredients with hand beater or fork until blended; pour over bread pieces. Cook uncovered in 350° oven until puffy and golden brown, about 35 minutes.

Two-Bean Salad

½ can (8-ounce size) cut green beans
    (about ½ cup drained)
½ can (8-ounce size) red kidney beans
    (about ⅓ cup drained)
¼ cup bottled Italian dressing
1 tablespoon chopped green pepper
1 tablespoon chopped onion
1 teaspoon sugar
  Lettuce cup

Toss all ingredients except lettuce cup. Cover and refrigerate at least 4 hours. Drain; spoon into lettuce cup.

Grenadine Sundae

Drizzle grenadine syrup over scoop of vanilla ice cream.

VEGETABLE MEAT LOAF
CHEESY BAKED POTATO
ORANGE AND ONION SALAD

Vegetable Meat Loaf

¼ pound ground beef
½ slice bread, torn into small pieces
    (about ¼ cup)*
1 egg yolk or white
2 tablespoons shredded carrot
1 tablespoon chopped onion
1 tablespoon chopped green pepper
1 tablespoon chopped celery
1 tablespoon chili sauce or catsup
¼ teaspoon salt
    Dash each of pepper and garlic powder
1 tablespoon chili sauce or catsup

Mix all ingredients except 1 tablespoon chili sauce. Shape mixture into loaf, 3x2½ inches, in ungreased shallow baking pan. Spoon 1 tablespoon chili sauce over loaf. Cook uncovered in 350° oven until done, about 45 minutes.

*1 tablespoon plus 1 teaspoon dry bread crumbs, 1 tablespoon plus 1 teaspoon wheat germ or 2 tablespoons oats can be substituted for the bread pieces.

Basic Meat Loaf: Omit carrot, green pepper and celery.

Cheesy Baked Potato

1 medium potato
    Margarine or butter
1 to 2 tablespoons shredded pasteurized
    process cheese spread loaf

Prick potato with fork to allow steam to escape. If desired, rub with shortening for softer skin. Cook in 350° oven until soft, 1¼ to 1½ hours.

Cut crisscross gash in top; squeeze gently until some potato pops up through opening. Top with margarine and cheese.

To Microwave: Prick 1 medium potato with fork to allow steam to escape. Place in microwave. Microwave uncovered on high (full) power until tender, 11 to 13 minutes. Let stand 1 minute.

Orange and Onion Salad

    Honey Dressing (below)
1 thin slice Bermuda onion, separated
    into rings
1 orange, pared, sliced and slices cut into
    halves
    Lettuce leaves

Prepare Honey Dressing; pour over onion rings. Cover and refrigerate at least 1 hour.

Remove onion rings with slotted spoon. Arrange onion rings and orange pieces on lettuce leaves; spoon dressing over salad.

HONEY DRESSING

1 tablespoon vegetable oil
1 teaspoon snipped parsley
1 teaspoon lemon juice
1 teaspoon honey
    Dash of salt

Shake all ingredients in tightly covered jar.

Ground Beef Pasty

PICKLED BEETS
DILL PICKLES
NUTTY PEACH DESSERT

(menu box header)

GROUND BEEF PASTY
PICKLED BEETS
DILL PICKLES
NUTTY PEACH DESSERT

Ground Beef Pasty

   Pastry (below)
¼ pound ground beef, crumbled
¼ cup chopped potato
¼ cup chopped carrot
 2 tablespoons chopped onion
¼ teaspoon salt
⅛ teaspoon pepper
   Milk

Prepare Pastry; roll into 10-inch circle on lightly floured cloth-covered board with floured stockinet-covered rolling pin. Place on ungreased cookie sheet. Place beef, potato, carrot and onion on half of the circle to within 1 inch of edge; sprinkle with salt and pepper.

Brush edge of pastry with water. Fold pastry over filling; fold bottom edge of pastry over top edge of pastry. Press edges with a fork to seal. Make slits in top of pastry; brush with milk. Bake in 350° oven until golden brown, about 1 hour. Serve with chili sauce if desired.

PASTRY

 3 tablespoons shortening
½ cup all-purpose flour
¼ teaspoon salt
 1 to 2 tablespoons cold water

Cut shortening into flour and salt until particles are size of small peas. Sprinkle in water, 1 teaspoon at a time, tossing with fork until all flour is moistened and pastry almost cleans side of bowl. Gather pastry into a ball.

Pickled Beets

 1 can (8¼ ounces) sliced beets, drained
   (reserve liquid)
¼ cup vinegar
½ cup sugar
 1 small cinnamon stick

Add enough water to reserved liquid to measure ½ cup. Heat liquid mixture, vinegar, sugar and cinnamon stick to boiling, stirring occasionally. Place beets in glass bowl; pour liquid mixture over beets. Cover and refrigerate at least 4 hours. Serve on lettuce leaves if desired.

Nutty Peach Dessert

 2 canned peach halves
 1 teaspoon lemon juice
½ bar (1.4-ounce size) salted nut roll,
   chopped

Place peach halves in ungreased 10-ounce casserole or custard cup. Drizzle with lemon juice. Sprinkle with salted nut roll. Cook uncovered in 350° oven until peach halves are hot, about 10 minutes.

Should Know...

If you enjoy an occasional cookie or candy for dessert or a snack, there is no need to overeat or waste. Most candy stays fresh for a year or more if stored at 0° in freezer wrap. Both frosted and unfrosted cookies usually freeze well. (All cookies must be completely cooled before freezing.) If frosted, freeze on a flat surface until firm, then place in airtight containers or freezer-wrap "personalized" amounts. Unfrosted cookies can be packed and frozen immediately after cooling. Figure on 20 to 30 minutes thawing time at room temperature for cookies; candies depend on individual taste.

Fold pastry over filling almost to bottom edge. Fold bottom edge over top edge to seal.

Crimp edges with a fork, then cut slits in pastry and brush with milk.

OVEN-FRIED CHICKEN
CHEESE-GRITS PUFF
SPICED APPLES
SWEET-AND-SOUR
CABBAGE SLAW
DESSERT FONDUE

Oven-fried Chicken

1 tablespoon all-purpose flour
⅛ teaspoon salt
⅛ teaspoon paprika
  Dash of pepper
1 chicken leg or thigh
1 tablespoon margarine or butter
1 tablespoon vegetable oil

Mix flour, salt, paprika and pepper. Coat chicken with flour mixture. Heat margarine and oil in 6-inch ovenproof skillet or baking pan, 8x8x2 inches, in 350° oven until margarine is melted. Place coated chicken, skin side down, in skillet. Cook uncovered 30 minutes. Turn chicken; cook uncovered until chicken is done, about 30 minutes longer.

Cheese-Grits Puff

¾ cup water
3 tablespoons quick-cooking hominy
   grits
2 tablespoons shredded pasteurized
   process cheese spread loaf
1 egg white, slightly beaten
1 tablespoon margarine or butter
½ teaspoon seasoned salt
  Paprika

Heat water to boiling. Gradually stir in grits. Heat to boiling. Reduce heat; cook uncovered, stirring occasionally, until thick, 2 to 3 minutes. Stir in cheese, egg white, margarine and seasoned salt. Pour into ungreased 10-ounce casserole or custard cup; sprinkle with paprika. Cook uncovered in 350° oven until firm and cracks are dry, about 30 minutes.

Sweet-and-Sour Cabbage Slaw

  Sweet-and-Sour Dressing (below)
1 cup shredded cabbage
2 green onions (with tops), sliced
1 small carrot, shredded

Prepare Sweet-and-Sour Dressing; toss with remaining ingredients.

SWEET-AND-SOUR DRESSING

1 tablespoon honey
1 tablespoon peach or apricot preserves
1 teaspoon vinegar

Mix all ingredients.

Dessert Fondue

¼ cup boiling water
¼ package (3-ounce size) fruit-flavored
   gelatin (about 1 tablespoon plus
   2 teaspoons)
  Bite-size pieces angel food or
   pound cake
  Whipped topping, chopped nuts or
   coconut

Pour boiling water on gelatin in small bowl; stir until gelatin is dissolved. Spear angel food cake with fork; dip into gelatin. Dip into whipped topping.

Note: To prepare individual ½-cup serving fruit-flavored gelatin, pour ¼ cup boiling water on about 1 tablespoon plus 1 teaspoon gelatin; stir until gelatin is dissolved. Stir in ¼ cup cold water. Refrigerate until firm, about 3 hours.

CHICKEN IN FOIL
CONFETTI COTTAGE CHEESE
DROP BISCUITS
ROSY APPLE

Chicken in Foil

1 chicken leg or thigh
1 medium potato, cut into fourths
1 medium carrot, cut into ¼-inch slices
1 envelope individual serving instant
    cream of chicken soup
1 envelope individual serving instant
    onion soup
½ cup water
½ cup frozen cut green beans

Place chicken in center of piece of aluminum foil, 18x15 inches. Place potato on 1 side of chicken; place carrot on other side. Mix instant soups and water until thickened. Spoon over chicken; top with green beans. Wrap securely in foil; place on ungreased cookie sheet. Cook in 450° oven until chicken is done, about 50 minutes.

Beef in Foil: Substitute 4-ounce piece beef boneless round steak, about ½ inch thick, for the chicken leg or thigh. Cook in 450° oven until beef is tender, 50 to 60 minutes.

Confetti Cottage Cheese

½ cup creamed cottage cheese
1 tablespoon thinly sliced celery
1 tablespoon chopped radish
1 teaspoon snipped parsley
    Dash each of onion salt, seasoned salt
      and pepper
    Lettuce leaves

Mix all ingredients except lettuce leaves. Cover and refrigerate at least 1 hour but no longer than 24 hours. Serve on lettuce leaves.

Drop Biscuits

Heat oven to 450°. Mix ½ cup buttermilk baking mix and 3 tablespoons milk with fork until soft dough forms. Drop by spoonfuls onto ungreased cookie sheet or double thickness aluminum foil. Bake until golden brown, 8 to 10 minutes. 2 biscuits.

Rosy Apple

1 medium baking apple
1 tablespoon packed brown sugar
1 teaspoon margarine or butter
1 tablespoon grenadine syrup
1 tablespoon water

Core apple; pare upper third of apple to prevent skin from splitting. Place apple upright in ungreased 10-ounce casserole or custard cup. Fill center of apple with brown sugar; top with margarine. Pour grenadine syrup over apple. Spoon water into casserole around apple. Cook in 450° oven until apple is fork-tender, 20 to 30 minutes (time will vary with size and variety of apple). Serve warm with ice cream if desired.

1 Should Know...

Think of cottage cheese as an inexpensive meat stretcher or meat substitute. With ½ cup of creamed cottage cheese, you can provide the protein equivalent of a 2-ounce portion of cooked meat, poultry or fish, 2 eggs or 2 slices of Cheddar cheese. And, the calories are low: 120 in ½ cup of creamed cottage cheese (4% milk fat); 90 to 100 in low-fat varieties (between 0.5% and 2% milk fat). Refrigerate promptly and use within a few days. Dry cottage cheese can be frozen up to 1 month. Don't freeze creamed cottage cheese; it separates as it thaws.

Fish-stuffed Tomato

1 large tomato
   Dash each of salt and pepper
2 teaspoons soft bread crumbs
1 fish fillet (about 4 ounces)
1 teaspoon margarine or butter,
   softened
   Dash each of salt and pepper
¼ cup soft bread crumbs
2 teaspoons snipped parsley
2 teaspoons margarine or butter, melted
½ teaspoon instant minced onion
1½ teaspoons lemon juice
   Dash each of salt, ground thyme,
    ground savory and pepper

Cut slice from top of tomato. Remove pulp, leaving a ¼-inch wall. Place tomato, cut side down, on wire rack to drain. Sprinkle inside of tomato with salt, pepper and 2 teaspoons bread crumbs. Brush fish fillet with margarine; sprinkle with salt and pepper. Mix remaining ingredients; spread on fish fillet. Roll up; place in tomato. Place tomato in ungreased 12-ounce custard cup. Cook uncovered in 350° oven until fish flakes easily with fork, about 30 minutes.

Broccoli with Cheese Sauce

2 spears broccoli
2 slices process American cheese
1 tablespoon milk
   Dash of onion salt
1 drop red pepper sauce, if desired

Heat 1 inch salted water (½ teaspoon salt to 1 cup water) to boiling. Add broccoli. Cover and heat to boiling. Cook until stems are tender, about 8 minutes; drain.

Heat remaining ingredients over medium heat, stirring frequently, until cheese is melted and mixture is smooth, about 4 minutes. Pour cheese sauce over broccoli.

Apple Turnover

   Pastry (below)
⅓ cup thinly sliced apple
2 teaspoons sugar
2 teaspoons flour
   Dash each of ground nutmeg, ground
    cinnamon and salt
1 teaspoon margarine or butter

Heat oven to 400°. Prepare Pastry; roll into 6-inch circle with floured sockinet-covered rolling pin. Mix remaining ingredients except margarine. Spoon apple mixture onto half of the pastry circle to within ½ inch of edge; dot with margarine. Fold pastry over filling; press edges with fork to seal. Brush with milk and sprinkle with sugar if desired. Bake on ungreased cookie sheet until golden brown, about 20 minutes.

PASTRY

2 tablespoons shortening
⅓ cup all-purpose flour
   Dash of salt
2 to 3 teaspoons water

Cut shortening into flour and salt until particles are size of small peas. Sprinkle in water, 1 teaspoon at a time, tossing with fork until all flour is moistened and pastry almost cleans side of bowl. Gather pastry into a ball; shape into flattened round on lightly floured cloth-covered board.

I CAN GIVE THE BUDGET A BREAK

Tailor-made for budget watchers — Fish-stuffed Tomato, Broccoli with Cheese Sauce and Apple Turnover (all recipes on page 38). Add Salty Breadsticks (page 94) for an extra treat.

Fish Stew

¼ cup chopped onion
2 tablespoons sliced celery
1 teaspoon margarine or butter
1 can (8 ounces) stewed tomatoes
¾ cup water
1 teaspoon instant chicken bouillon
1 teaspoon snipped parsley
½ teaspoon lemon juice
1 small bay leaf
⅛ teaspoon dried thyme leaves
  Dash of garlic powder
⅕ package (16-ounce size) frozen skinless
    haddock or cod fillets

Cook and stir onion and celery in margarine in 1-quart saucepan over medium heat until onion is tender, about 3 minutes. Stir in tomatoes, water, instant bouillon, parsley, lemon juice, bay leaf, thyme and garlic powder. Heat to boiling. Reduce heat; simmer uncovered, stirring occasionally, 15 minutes. Cut piece of fish into ½-inch cubes; stir into tomato mixture. Simmer uncovered until fish flakes easily with fork, about 5 minutes. Remove bay leaf before serving.

Note: Use a sharp knife to cut frozen haddock. Store remaining frozen haddock in sealed package in freezer.

Mini Cheese Loaf

1 hard roll
1 tablespoon margarine or butter,
    softened
  Seasoned salt
2 tablespoons shredded pasteurized
    process cheese spread loaf

Cut roll into 3 equal slices almost through to bottom. Spread cut sides of roll with margarine; sprinkle with seasoned salt. Divide cheese between slices. Wrap in piece of aluminum foil, 12x8 inches. Place on ungreased cookie sheet. Heat in 400° oven until hot, 10 to 12 minutes.

Lemon Pudding

½ cup sugar
1 tablespoon cornstarch
½ cup water
1 egg yolk, slightly beaten
1 tablespoon margarine or butter
½ teaspoon grated lemon peel
3 tablespoons lemon juice

Mix sugar and cornstarch in 1-quart saucepan; gradually stir in water. Heat over medium heat, stirring constantly, until mixture thickens and boils. Boil and stir 1 minute. Gradually stir about half of the hot mixture into egg yolk. Stir egg yolk mixture into remaining hot mixture in saucepan. Heat to boiling, stirring constantly. Boil and stir 1 minute. Remove from heat; stir in remaining ingredients. Refrigerate until chilled.

When Your Freezer Comes To The Rescue

"What's so great about having a freezer—and the time to cook for it? I always seem to end up with enough to feed an army."

There's more than one way to make the most of your freezer—and your time. For the solo cook, the "most" should mean the most variety, not the most food.

Here you'll find six basic freezer mixes to prepare, divide and freeze whenever you please; then use them later to make 25 easy main dishes. Each one different. Just take your freezer mix, make a few last-minute additions and you have a new dish ready to go. Example: A single portion of Freezer

Chicken with Broth can be turned into Chicken Gumbo, Chicken a la King, Chicken Tetrazzini or Creamed Chicken and Broccoli Soup. The other mixes feature ground beef, pork and crepes.

So when the mood strikes, enjoy a creative cooking spree—and reap the benefits whenever you like.

Freezer Pork Cubes

1 pound pork boneless shoulder, cut into
    1-inch cubes
1 teaspoon salt
¼ teaspoon pepper
⅛ teaspoon garlic salt
1 cup water

Cook and stir pork in 8-inch skillet over medium heat until brown, 10 to 15 minutes. Sprinkle with salt, pepper and garlic salt; stir in water. Heat to boiling. Reduce heat; cover and simmer until pork is tender, 1 to 1¼ hours.

Drain pork; arrange pork in single layer in ungreased baking pan, 8x8x2 inches. Freeze uncovered 30 minutes. (This partial freezing prevents pork from freezing together solidly.)

Divide partially frozen pork into 4 portions (about ½ cup each). Wrap and label; freeze no longer than 2 months. Use Freezer Pork Cubes in the recipes that follow.

Pork-Cauliflower Combo

1 container frozen Freezer Pork Cubes*
⅓ cup cauliflowerets
¼ cup frozen green peas
¼ cup water
1 tablespoon chopped onion
1 teaspoon instant chicken bouillon
1 teaspoon shredded Cheddar or Swiss
    cheese
    Dried dill weed

Heat pork, cauliflowerets, peas, water, onion and instant bouillon to boiling in 1-quart saucepan. Reduce heat; cover and simmer, stirring occasionally, until pork is hot and cauliflowerets are tender, 10 to 15 minutes. Drain; sprinkle with cheese and dill weed.

Menu mates: Blue Cheese Tossed Salad (page 62) and lemon sherbet.

*½ cup ¾-inch cooked pork cubes can be substituted for the Freezer Pork Cubes.

Pork and Sauerkraut

½ can (8-ounce size) sauerkraut
    (about ½ cup)
1 small apple, cut into 12 wedges, or
    1 can (8 ounces) sliced peaches,
    drained
2 teaspoons packed brown sugar
1 container frozen Freezer Pork Cubes*

Layer half each of the sauerkraut and apple wedges in ungreased 20-ounce casserole. Sprinkle with 1 teaspoon of the brown sugar. Place pork on top. Layer with remaining sauerkraut and apple wedges; sprinkle with remaining 1 teaspoon brown sugar. Cover and cook in 375° oven until pork is hot, 20 to 25 minutes.

Menu mates: Parsleyed New Potatoes (page 86) and Two-Bean Salad (page 32).

*½ cup ¾-inch cooked pork cubes can be substituted for the Freezer Pork Cubes.

Safari Pork

2 onion slices
2 tablespoons uncooked regular rice
1 tablespoon margarine or butter
⅓ cup water
1 container frozen Freezer Pork Cubes*
3 prunes, cut into pieces, or 1 tablespoon raisins
1 teaspoon honey
½ teaspoon instant chicken bouillon
⅛ teaspoon curry powder
Dash each of ground ginger and ground cinnamon

Cook and stir onion and rice in margarine in 1-quart saucepan over medium heat until onion is tender, about 5 minutes; stir in remaining ingredients. Heat to boiling, stirring occasionally. Reduce heat; cover and simmer 14 minutes. (Do not lift cover or stir.) Remove pan from heat. Fluff pork mixture lightly with fork; cover and let steam 5 to 10 minutes.

Menu mates: Sesame Cucumber Salad (page 74) and Fruit and Cheese (page 86).

*½ cup ¾-inch cooked pork cubes can be substituted for the Freezer Pork Cubes.

Orange-glazed Pork

1 container frozen Freezer Pork Cubes*
½ cup orange juice
1 tablespoon packed brown sugar
¼ teaspoon salt
1 tablespoon all-purpose flour
½ can (11-ounce size) mandarin orange segments (about ½ cup drained; reserve 2 tablespoons syrup)
½ can (2-ounce size) mushroom stems and pieces (about 2 tablespoons drained)
Steamed Rice (page 69)
1 green onion (with top), sliced

Heat pork, orange juice, brown sugar and salt to boiling in 1-quart saucepan. Reduce heat; cover and simmer, stirring occasionally, until pork is hot, about 10 minutes.

Shake flour and reserved orange syrup in tightly covered jar; stir into pork mixture. Heat to boiling; boil and stir 1 minute. Carefully stir in orange segments and mushrooms. Serve over rice; sprinkle with green onion.

Menu mates: Tossed Greens and Croutons (page 72) and chocolate ice cream.

*½ cup ¾-inch cooked pork cubes can be substituted for the Freezer Pork Cubes.

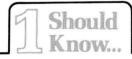 Should Know...

All cooked meats must be cooled quickly before freezing. This goes for unadorned leftovers as well as combination-type dishes. When completely chilled, wrap, label and freeze. At 0°, cooked meats can be frozen up to 2 months. Uncooked meats are another story: Most pork cuts can be kept 4 to 5 months. Ground pork and pork sausage, however, should be frozen no longer than 2 months. Ham slices, bacon and franks can be frozen but do lose quality. And lamb and veal cuts can be frozen 6 to 9 months. (See pages 46 and 48 for beef freezing tips.)

Be sure to label: contents, amount and maximum storage date.

CAN BANK ON THE FREEZER

Stock up ahead of time (when you have the time) and your dividends will come through when you need them. Beef-Tomato Freezer Mix pays off with Lentil Stew, Chili Con Carne and Stuffed Green Peppers (all recipes on pages 45 and 46).

Beef-Tomato Freezer Mix

1 pound ground beef
½ cup chopped onion
¼ cup chopped green pepper
1 small clove garlic, finely chopped
1 can (8 ounces) tomato sauce
¼ cup catsup
½ teaspoon salt
¼ teaspoon pepper

Cook and stir beef, onion, green pepper and garlic in 8-inch skillet over medium heat until beef is brown; drain. Stir in remaining ingredients. Heat to boiling. Reduce heat; cover and simmer, stirring occasionally, 10 minutes.

Divide mixture among four 1-pint freezer containers (about ½ cup each); cool quickly. Cover and label; freeze no longer than 3 months. Use Beef-Tomato Freezer Mix in the recipes that follow below and on page 46.

Lentil Stew

1 container frozen Beef-Tomato Freezer Mix
¾ cup water
2 tablespoons uncooked lentils
1 tablespoon snipped parsley
1 small carrot, sliced
1 small stalk celery, sliced
½ jar (2½-ounce size) sliced mushrooms (about 2 tablespoons drained)
Dash of salt

Dip container of frozen mix into hot water just to loosen. Heat frozen mix, water, lentils and parsley to boiling in 1-quart saucepan. Reduce heat; cover and simmer, stirring occasionally, 20 minutes. Stir in remaining ingredients. Heat to boiling. Reduce heat; cover and simmer until vegetables are tender, about 20 minutes.

Menu mates: Waldorf Salad (page 14) and a rye hard roll.

Italian Spaghetti

1 container frozen Beef-Tomato Freezer Mix
½ cup water
1 tablespoon catsup
1 tablespoon snipped parsley
⅛ teaspoon dried oregano leaves
Dash each of dried sweet basil and garlic powder
1 cup hot cooked spaghetti

Dip container of frozen mix into hot water just to loosen. Heat frozen mix, water, catsup, parsley, oregano, basil and garlic powder to boiling in 1-quart saucepan. Reduce heat; cover and simmer, stirring occasionally, until mix is thawed, 5 to 8 minutes. Simmer uncovered until desired thickness, about 10 minutes. Serve over spaghetti.

Menu mates: Antipasto Vegetable Salad (page 64) and breadsticks.

Chili Con Carne

1 container frozen Beef-Tomato Freezer
    Mix
⅓ cup water
½ can (8-ounce size) kidney beans
    (about ½ cup)
½ to 1 teaspoon chili powder

Dip container of frozen mix into hot water just to loosen. Heat frozen mix and water to boiling in 1-quart saucepan. Reduce heat; cover and simmer, stirring occasionally, until thawed, 5 to 8 minutes. Stir in kidney beans (with liquid) and chili powder. Heat to boiling. Reduce heat; simmer uncovered until desired consistency, about 15 minutes.

Menu mates: Cornmeal Muffins (page 79) and Melon Sundae (page 24).

Stuffed Green Pepper

1 medium green pepper
1 container frozen Beef-Tomato Freezer
    Mix
⅓ cup water
2 tablespoons uncooked instant rice
¼ teaspoon salt
⅛ teaspoon Worcestershire sauce

Cut thin slice from stem end of green pepper; remove seeds and membrane. Wash inside and outside. Cook green pepper in 3 cups boiling salted water 5 minutes; drain.

Dip container of frozen mix into hot water just to loosen. Heat frozen mix, water, rice, salt and Worcestershire sauce to boiling in 1-quart saucepan. Reduce heat; cover and simmer, stirring occasionally, until mix is thawed, 5 to 8 minutes.

Place green pepper, cut side up, in ungreased 20-ounce casserole. Spoon beef mixture into green pepper. Cover and cook in 350° oven until hot and rice is tender, about 30 minutes. Garnish with tomato wedges if desired.

Menu mates: Grape Toss (page 19) and Chocolate-Peanut Butter Sundae (page 92).

1 Should Know...

Take advantage of beef "specials" even if prepackaged portions are larger than you'd normally buy. You can safely freeze all beef at 0°, but storage time does vary from cut to cut. Here's a timetable:

Steaks, roasts (most cuts)	9 months
Chunks (for stewing)	4 months
Liver, heart, tongue	6 months
Ground	3-4 months
Meat loaf (cooked or uncooked)	1 month
Cooked	2 months

If you're planning to freezer-store prepackaged meat longer than 2 weeks, you'll have to rewrap. Wrap tightly in moistureproof, vaporproof wrap, pressing out all the air. Layer wrap between steaks, chops and patties for easier separating.

Ground Beef Freezer Mix

1 pound ground beef
½ cup chopped onion
1 small clove garlic, finely chopped
½ teaspoon salt
¼ teaspoon pepper

Cook and stir beef, onion and garlic over medium heat until beef is brown; drain. Stir in salt and pepper. Spread mixture in ungreased baking pan 8x8x2 inches. Freeze 1 hour. (This partial freezing prevents beef from freezing together solidly.)

Crumble partially frozen beef mixture into small pieces. Divide into 4 portions (about ¾ cup each). Wrap and label; freeze no longer than 3 months. Use Ground Beef Freeer Mix in the recipes that follow below and on page 48.

Mexican Casserole

¼ cup buttermilk baking mix
1 tablespoon water
1 container frozen Ground Beef Freezer
    Mix
1 tomato slice
1 tablespoon chopped green pepper
3 tablespoons dairy sour cream
1 tablespoon mayonnaise or salad
    dressing
    Paprika

Mix baking mix and water until soft dough forms. Press dough in bottom and ½ inch up side of 10-ounce casserole or custard cup. Layer half of the frozen mix, the tomato, green pepper and remaining frozen mix in casserole. Mix sour cream and mayonnaise; spread over frozen mix. Sprinkle with paprika. Cook uncovered in 350° oven until beef is hot and top is light brown, about 30 minutes.

Menu mates: Avocado Salad (page 68) and Mocha Coffee (page 31).

Beef Noodle Dish

1 container frozen Ground Beef Freezer
    Mix
¾ cup water
1 envelope individual serving instant
    onion soup
¼ cup frozen green peas
¼ cup uncooked noodles
    (about 1 ounce)
1 teaspoon chopped pimiento
1 teaspoon water
2 teaspoons all-purpose flour

Heat frozen mix, water, instant soup, peas, noodles and pimiento to boiling in 1-quart saucepan. Reduce heat; cover and simmer, stirring occasionally, until beef is hot and noodles are tender, 5 to 7 minutes.

Shake water and flour in tightly covered jar; stir into beef mixture. Heat to boiling, stirring constantly. Boil and stir 1 minute.

Menu mates: Orange and Onion Salad (page 33) and a chocolate brownie.

Greek Beef and Potato

1 container frozen Ground Beef Freezer
   Mix
¼ cup cocktail vegetable juice or tomato
   juice
2 tablespoons catsup
1 tablespoon snipped parsley
   Dash of ground nutmeg
1 small potato, cut into ⅛-inch slices
1 egg white
1 tablespoon water
   Paprika
   Grated Parmesan cheese
   Snipped parsley

Heat frozen mix, juice, catsup, 1 tablespoon parsley and the nutmeg to boiling in 1-quart saucepan. Reduce heat; cover and simmer, stirring occasionally, until beef is hot, about 10 minutes. Layer half each of the potato slices and beef mixture in ungreased 15- or 16-ounce casserole or custard cup; repeat. Cover and cook in 375° oven until potato is tender, about 30 minutes.

Mix egg white and water; pour over beef mixture. Sprinkle with paprika. Cook uncovered until egg is set, about 5 minutes. Sprinkle with cheese and parsley.

Menu mates: Buttered green beans and Minty Lemon Sherbet (page 18).

Open-face Sloppy Joe

1 container frozen Ground Beef Freezer
   Mix
¼ cup catsup
2 tablespoons water
2 tablespoons chopped celery
1 teaspoon packed brown sugar
1 hamburger bun, split and toasted

Heat frozen mix, catsup, water, celery and brown sugar to boiling in 1-quart saucepan. Reduce heat; cover and simmer, stirring occasionally, until beef is hot, about 10 minutes. Serve on bun halves; garnish with canned French fried onions if desired.

Menu mates: Pickles and Fresh Fruit Slush (page 16).

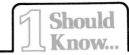
I Should Know...

If you plan to keep ground beef more than 24 hours before using, you must freeze it. Freeze meal-size portions tightly wrapped in moistureproof, vaporproof wrap up to 4 months at 0°. Or prepare the meat according to how you ultimately plan to use it and then freeze.

For burgers: Shape into patties and wrap individually in heavy-duty or double thickness aluminum foil. Or stack with a double layer of aluminum foil or freezer wrap between each patty; then overwrap.

For meatballs: Prepare mixture and shape according to your favorite recipe. Place in ungreased shallow baking pan and freeze uncovered 3 hours. (This keeps the meatballs from freezing together.) Pack meal-size amounts in heavy plastic bags or freezer containers or wrap in heavy-duty or double thickness aluminum foil.

Freezer Meatballs

1 pound ground beef
½ cup dry bread crumbs or 3 slices bread,
   torn into small pieces
¼ cup milk
2 tablespoons chopped onion
1 teaspoon salt
½ teaspoon Worcestershire sauce
   Dash of pepper
1 egg

Mix all ingredients. Shape mixture into thirty 1¼-inch balls. Place in ungreased jelly roll pan, 15½x10½x1 inch. Cook uncovered in 400° oven until done, about 10 minutes. Cool 5 minutes. Freeze uncovered 15 minutes. (This partial freezing prevents meatballs from freezing together solidly.)

Divide partially frozen meatballs among 5 freezer containers (6 meatballs each). Cover and label; freeze no longer than 2 months. Use freezer meatballs in the recipes that follow below and on pages 50-51.

Meatball Stew

1 envelope (about ¾ ounce) brown gravy
   mix
1 cup water
1 small carrot, cut into 1-inch pieces
1 small stalk celery, cut into 1-inch
   pieces
1 small potato, cut into 1-inch pieces
1 container frozen Freezer Meatballs

Mix gravy mix and water in 1-quart saucepan; add carrot, celery and potato. Heat to boiling. Reduce heat; cover and simmer, stirring occasionally, 25 minutes. Add meatballs; cover and simmer, stirring occasionally, until meatballs are hot and vegetables are tender, about 15 minutes.

Menu mate: Orange-Apple Salad (page 17).

Saucy Meatballs

1 container frozen Freezer Meatballs
1 envelope individual serving instant
   cream of chicken soup
¾ cup water
   Dash of ground nutmeg
2 tablespoons dairy sour cream
   Hot cooked rice or mashed potatoes
   Snipped parsley

Mix meatballs, instant soup, water and nutmeg in 1-quart saucepan. Heat to boiling. Reduce heat; cover and simmer, stirring occasionally, until meatballs are hot, about 15 minutes. Stir in sour cream; heat through. Serve over rice; sprinkle with parsley.

Menu mates: Pickled Beets (page 34), celery sticks and Honey-Wine Peaches (page 16).

Country-style Meatballs

2 slices onion
1 tablespoon margarine or butter
1 container frozen Freezer Meatballs
⅓ cup dry red wine or tomato juice
⅓ cup water
4 mushrooms, sliced
1 teaspoon instant beef bouillon
¼ teaspoon paprika
⅛ teaspoon caraway seed
⅛ teaspoon salt
2 tablespoons water
2 tablespoons all-purpose flour
   Hot cooked rice or noodles

Cook and stir onion in margarine in 1-quart saucepan over medium heat until onion is tender, about 5 minutes. Stir in meatballs, wine, ⅓ cup water, the mushrooms, instant bouillon, paprika, caraway seed and salt. Heat to boiling. Reduce heat; cover and simmer, stirring occasionally, until meatballs are hot, about 15 minutes. Shake 2 tablespoons water and the flour in tightly covered jar; stir into meatball mixture. Heat to boiling, stirring constantly. Boil and stir 1 minute. Serve over rice.

Menu mates: Artichoke Salad (page 15) and fresh fruit.

1 Should Know...

All ground beef is not the same. Federal laws specify the amount of fat permitted in the various types of ground beef, so it is actually the amount of fat that determines the label.

Hamburger: Any ground beef bearing this label can legally contain up to 30 percent fat. And this fat may consist of the natural fat attached to the beef plus "loose" beef fat.

Ground Beef: Here the amount of fat may also be 30 percent. However, only the fat attached to the cut of beef being ground may be used; no other beef fat can be added.

Lean Ground Beef (ground chuck): The fat level in ground beef bearing this label is 20 percent or less.

Extra Lean Ground Beef (ground round): This type of ground beef usually contains about 15 percent fat.

Sauerbraten Meatballs

1 container frozen Freezer Meatballs
½ cup water
2 gingersnaps, crushed (about
    2 tablespoons)
1 tablespoon raisins
1 tablespoon vinegar
1 teaspoon packed brown sugar
½ teaspoon instant beef bouillon
    Dash of pepper
    Hot cooked noodles or boiled potatoes

Heat meatballs, water, gingersnaps, raisins, vinegar, brown sugar, instant bouillon and pepper to boiling in 1-quart saucepan. Reduce heat; cover and simmer, stirring occasionally, until meatballs are hot, about 15 minutes. Serve over noodles.

Menu mates: Chive-buttered Carrots (page 94) and Apple Slaw (page 31).

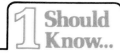
Should Know...

Give pasta a permanent place in your cupboard. You'll want to stock macaroni, spaghetti and noodles (save some shelf space for personal favorites like lasagne). And since you can cook just the amount you'll need, there's seldom any waste—that's good news for any single-person household.

For a single serving (1 cup) of cooked pasta, you need 1½ to 2 ounces or ½ cup uncooked macaroni; 1½ to 2 ounces uncooked spaghetti; 2 ounces or 1 cup uncooked egg noodles. To keep drained cooked pasta from sticking together, toss with 1 tablespoon margarine or butter.

Barbecued Macaroni and Meatballs

1 container frozen Freezer Meatballs
1 can (6 ounces) tomato juice (¾ cup)
1 tablespoon packed brown sugar
1 tablespoon catsup
1 tablespoon chopped onion
½ teaspoon lemon juice
⅛ teaspoon salt
4 to 6 drops pepper sauce
¼ cup uncooked macaroni

Heat meatballs, tomato juice, brown sugar, catsup, onion, lemon juice, salt and pepper sauce to boiling in 1-quart saucepan; stir in macaroni. Reduce heat; cover and simmer, stirring occasionally, until meatballs are hot and macaroni is tender, about 15 minutes.

Quick Barbecued Macaroni and Meatballs: Prepare as directed except—substitute ½ cup barbecue sauce and ⅓ cup water for the tomato juice, brown sugar, catsup, onion, lemon juice, salt and pepper sauce.

Menu mates: Buttered peas and Banana Pudding Parfait (page 84).

Freezer Chicken with Broth

2¼ pounds chicken legs with thighs
    (3 or 4 legs with thighs)
  1 carrot, cut up
  1 celery stalk, cut up
  1 sprig parsley
  1 teaspoon salt
 ¼ teaspoon pepper

Remove any excess fat from chicken. Place all ingredients in 3-quart saucepan. Add just enough water to cover. Heat to boiling. Reduce heat; cover and simmer until chicken is done, about 45 minutes.

Cool quickly. Remove chicken from bones and skin; cut into pieces. Divide chicken among four 1-pint freezer containers (about ⅓ cup each). Strain broth; pour ¾ cup broth into each container. Cover and label; freeze no longer than 6 months. Use Freezer Chicken with Broth in the recipes that follow below and on page 54.

Chicken Gumbo

  1 container frozen Freezer Chicken with
    Broth*
 ¼ package (10-ounce size) frozen cut okra
 ½ can (8-ounce size) stewed tomatoes
    (about ½ cup)
  6 to 8 drops red pepper sauce
 ¼ teaspoon salt
  1 small bay leaf
    Dash of pepper
    Quick Rice (page 67)

Dip container of frozen mix into hot water just to loosen. Heat frozen mix, okra, tomatoes, pepper sauce, salt, bay leaf and pepper to boiling in 1-quart saucepan. Reduce heat; cover and simmer, stirring occasionally, until chicken is hot, about 15 minutes. Remove bay leaf. Serve chicken mixture over rice.

Menu mates: Sesame breadsticks and Ginger Pear Parfait (page 65)

*⅓ cup cut-up cooked chicken and ¾ cup chicken broth can be substituted for the Freezer Chicken with Broth.

Chicken a la King

  1 container frozen Freezer Chicken with
    Broth*
 ½ cup frozen green peas
  1 envelope individual serving instant
    cream of chicken soup
  1 teaspoon chopped pimiento
    Toast, mashed potatoes, hot cooked
    rice or hot cooked noodles

Dip container of frozen mix into hot water just to loosen. Heat frozen mix and peas to boiling. Reduce heat; cover and simmer, stirring occasionally, until chicken is hot, about 15 minutes. Stir in soup and pimiento. Serve over toast.

Menu mates: Melon and Strawberries (page 26) with vanilla wafers.

*⅓ cup cut-up cooked chicken and ¾ cup chicken broth can be substituted for the Freezer Chicken with Broth. Decrease simmering time to about 8 minutes.

11 CAN COOK FOR THE FREEZER

With individual portions of
Freezer Chicken with Broth on
hand, you can take off in many
different directions: Chicken
Gumbo, Creamed Chicken and
Broccoli Soup, Chicken a la King
(all recipes on pages 52 and 54).

Chicken Tetrazzini

1 container frozen Freezer Chicken with Broth*

½ can (2-ounce size) mushroom stems and pieces (about 2 tablespoons drained)

½ cup uncooked broken thin spaghetti (about 1 ounce)

1 envelope individual serving instant cream of chicken soup

1 tablespoon dry white wine

1 teaspoon grated Parmesan cheese

Dip container of frozen mix into hot water just to loosen. Heat frozen mix to boiling in 1-quart saucepan. Reduce heat; cover and simmer, stirring occasionally, until chicken is hot, about 15 minutes. Stir in mushrooms, spaghetti, soup and wine. Heat to boiling. Pour into ungreased 20-ounce casserole. Cover and cook in 350° oven until spaghetti is tender, about 20 minutes. Stir; sprinkle with cheese.

Menu mates: Tomato-Olive Salad (page 84) and Rosy Apple (page 37).

*⅓ cup cut-up cooked chicken and ¾ cup chicken broth can be substituted for the Freezer Chicken with Broth. Heat to boiling; do not simmer.

Creamed Chicken and Broccoli Soup

1 container frozen Freezer Chicken with Broth*

¼ package (10-ounce size) frozen chopped broccoli

¼ cup half-and-half or milk

½ teaspoon seasoned salt

¼ teaspoon onion salt

1 teaspoon imitation bacon or 1 slice bacon, crisply fried and crumbled

Dip container of frozen mix into hot water just to loosen. Heat frozen mix and broccoli to boiling in 1-quart saucepan. Reduce heat; cover and simmer, stirring occasionally, until chicken is hot and broccoli is tender, about 15 minutes. Pour into blender container. Add half-and-half, seasoned salt and onion salt. Cover and blend on medium speed until chicken and broccoli are finely chopped, about 15 seconds. Pour into saucepan; heat until hot. Sprinkle with imitation bacon.

Menu mates: Mini Cheese Loaf (page 40) and Grapefruit Grenadine (page 93).

*⅓ cup cut-up cooked chicken and ¾ cup chicken broth can be substituted for the Freezer Chicken and Broth.

Note: Use a sharp knife to cut frozen broccoli. Store remaining frozen broccoli in sealed package in freezer.

To freeze poultry successfully, wash, pat dry and wrap tightly. It's important to stay within these storage limits at 0°:

Chicken or turkey parts	9 months
Cooked poultry	1 month
Cooked poultry in broth or gravy	6 months

Stuffing? Don't freeze at all. To thaw poultry, leave in its wrapping in the refrigerator (allow about 2 hours per pound).

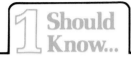

About Making Ordinary Breads Special

A go-with bread that's quick and easy to fix is a welcome touch for every meal. Choose from the wide variety of bakery breads available, and then try some of these easy fix-ups. And remember that freezing leftover breads will keep them fresh—up to 9 months for yeast breads, 2 to 3 months for quick breads.

Lemon English Muffin: Mix 1 tablespoon margarine or butter, softened, 1 teaspoon honey and ⅛ teaspoon grated lemon peel. Toast 1 English muffin. Spread margarine mixture over hot muffin halves.

Cheesy English Muffin: Set oven control to broil and/or 550°. Spread cut surfaces of an English muffin with margarine or butter, softened. Sprinkle with garlic salt and grated Parmesan cheese. Broil with tops 4 inches from heat until golden brown, 5 to 6 minutes.

Toasted Rye Bread: Spread 2 slices of rye bread with margarine or butter, softened; heat on ungreased cookie sheet in 325° oven until hot, about 10 minutes. Sprinkle with Parmesan cheese if desired.

Sesame Melba Triangles: Mix 1½ teaspoons margarine or butter, softened, ¾ teaspoon sesame seed and a dash of salt. Remove crusts from 2 bread slices; spread slices with margarine mixture. Cut slices into halves. Heat on ungreased cookie sheet in 350° oven until crisp, about 20 minutes.

Herbed Crusty Roll: Set oven control at broil and/or 550°. Split 1 hard roll horizontally. Spread halves with margarine or butter, softened, and sprinkle with Italian herb seasoning. Place on rack in broiler pan. Broil with tops 4 inches from heat until golden brown, about 4 minutes.

Herbed-topped Roll: Brush top of brown and serve roll with melted margarine or butter. Sprinkle with one of the following: parsley flakes, snipped chives, dill weed, onion salt, garlic salt. Bake on ungreased cookie sheet in 450° oven until golden brown, 10 to 12 minutes.

Garlic Bun Sticks: Split a frankfurter bun lengthwise into halves. Brush each half with margarine or butter, softened; sprinkle with garlic salt. Heat on ungreased cookie sheet in 350° oven until light brown, 10 to 12 minutes.

Breakfast Hot Sweets: Cut unsliced nut bread into desired number of ½-inch slices. Spread with margarine or butter, softened. Place buttered sides down on ungreased cookie sheet. Bake in 400° oven until light brown, 6 to 8 minutes.

Jam Grill: Spread 1 slice bread with 2 tablespoons strawberry or raspberry jam; top with second slice bread. Spread outside of sandwich with about 1 tablespoon margarine or butter, softened. Cook on both sides in skillet or on grill. Sprinkle with confectioners' sugar.

Jam Crumpets: Spread cut surfaces of English muffin halves with 1 teaspoon each margarine or butter, softened, and jam. Sprinkle with brown sugar and coconut. Bake on ungreased cookie sheet in 450° oven until bubbly and brown, about 5 minutes.

Freezer Crepes

¾ cup all-purpose flour
1½ teaspoons sugar
¼ teaspoon baking powder
¼ teaspoon salt
1 cup milk
1 egg
1 tablespoon vegetable oil

Beat all ingredients with hand beater until smooth. Lightly butter 7- or 8-inch skillet; heat over medium heat until butter is bubbly. Pour scant ¼ cup batter into skillet; rotate skillet until batter covers bottom. Cook until light brown; turn and cook other side until light brown. Repeat with remaining batter.

Stack crepes, placing waxed paper between them. Keep crepes covered to prevent them from drying out. Divide crepes into 4 pairs. Wrap and label; freeze no longer than 3 months. Use Freezer Crepes in the recipes that follow below and on page 58.

Note: To thaw Freezer Crepes, remove from freezer, unwrap and separate. Let stand at room temperature until soft, about 15 minutes.

Vegetable-Cheese Crepes

2 onion slices
1 tablespoon margarine or butter
1 small zucchini or yellow squash, sliced
5 medium mushrooms, sliced
½ teaspoon salt
⅛ teaspoon garlic powder
½ medium tomato, chopped
1 package frozen Freezer Crepes, thawed*
¼ cup shredded Cheddar or Swiss cheese (about 2 ounces)
¼ cup alfalfa sprouts

Cook and stir onion in margarine in 8-inch skillet over medium heat until tender, about 3 minutes; stir in zucchini, mushrooms, salt and garlic powder. Cook uncovered over medium heat, stirring occasionally, until zucchini is crisp-tender, about 5 minutes; stir in tomato.

Place 1 crepe on heatproof plate or aluminum foil. Spoon half of the vegetable mixture onto half of crepe. Fold other half over vegetable mixture. Repeat with remaining crepe. Sprinkle with cheese. Set oven control to broil and/or 550°. Broil with tops about 3 inches from heat until cheese is melted, about 3 minutes. Top with alfalfa sprouts.

Menu mate: Mandarin Orange Sundae (page 21).

*Crepes (page 63) can be substituted for the Freezer Crepes.

Cook crepe until light brown on one side. Turn and cook other side until light brown.

To freeze, first stack crepes between sheets of waxed paper; then wrap with aluminum foil.

Cheese Pocket Crepes

3 tablespoons shredded Swiss or
    Cheddar cheese
2 slices bacon, crisply fried and
    crumbled, or 2 tablespoons finely
    chopped fully cooked smoked ham
½ teaspoon snipped chives or parsley
1 package frozen Freezer Crepes,
    thawed*
1 tablespoon margarine or butter

Spoon half each of the cheese, bacon and chives onto center of browner side of each crepe. Fold sides of crepes over filling; fold tops and bottoms of crepes, overlapping edges. Heat margarine in 8-inch skillet over medium heat until bubbly. Place crepes, seam sides down, in skillet. Cook, turning once, until golden brown, about 5 minutes. Serve with maple syrup or orange marmalade if desired.

Menu mates: Dilled Green Beans (page 21) and Avocado-Tomato Salad (page 16).

*Crepes (page 63) can be substituted for the Freezer Crepes.

German Beef Crepes

¼ pound ground beef
½ cup shredded cabbage
2 tablespoons chopped onion
2 tablespoons water
¼ teaspoon salt
⅛ teaspoon caraway seed
    Dash of pepper
1 package frozen Freezer Crepes*
    Chili sauce

Cook and stir beef in 8-inch skillet over medium heat until light brown; drain. Stir in cabbage, onion, water, salt, caraway seed and pepper. Heat to boiling. Reduce heat; cover and simmer, stirring occasionally, until cabbage is tender, about 10 minutes.

Heat frozen wrapped crepes in 350° oven until hot, about 10 minutes. Place 1 crepe on plate. Spoon half of the beef mixture onto half of crepe. Fold other half of crepe over beef mixture. Repeat with remaining crepe. Top with chili sauce.

Menu mates: Spiced apples and Lemon Pudding (page 40).

*Crepes (page 63) can be substituted for the Freezer Crepes.

Seafood Crepes

⅓ cup mayonnaise or salad dressing
2 tablespoons milk
½ can (8-ounce size) green beans (about ½
    cup drained)
¼ can (7¾-ounce size) salmon, flaked
    (about ¼ cup drained), or ¼ can
    (6½-ounce size) tuna (about ¼ cup
    drained)
1 package frozen Freezer Crepes,
    thawed*
¼ cup canned French fried onions

Mix mayonnaise and milk in 1-quart bowl until smooth; reserve 2 tablespoons. Stir green beans and salmon into remaining mayonnaise mixture in bowl. Place 1 crepe in ungreased pie plate, 9x1¼ inches. Spoon half of the salmon mixture down center of crepe. Fold sides of crepe over salmon mixture, overlapping edges. Repeat with remaining crepe. Spoon reserved mayonnaise mixture over crepes; sprinkle with onions. Heat uncovered in 350° oven until salmon mixture is hot, about 20 minutes.

Menu mates: Spinach-Banana Salad (page 25) and orange sherbet.

*Crepes (page 63) can be substituted for the Freezer Crepes.

Note: Refrigerate remaining salmon in tightly covered glass or plastic container. Store no longer than 3 days.

When The Day Calls For Something Special

"Fussing for guests is one thing, but I'd never think of fussing for myself."

Why not? Who deserves it more? There's no need to call in company as an excuse to celebrate or splurge. Set out the candles, linens and nicest china, and treat yourself to one of the following menus when you feel you deserve something special.

Entertain the idea of Stuffed Mushrooms nestled beside Bacon-wrapped Beef Tenderloin, and English Trifle for dessert. Or go Italian! Offer a cool Antipasto Vegetable Salad as the introduction to Spaghetti-Cheese Toss, with fruit for the finale.

The next time you feel like doing something nice for yourself, look to the following pages. Pull out all the stops and invite yourself to dinner . . . especially for one.

Herbed Lamb Chop

1 lamb loin, sirloin or rib chop, about
      ¾ inch thick
    Bottled oil and vinegar dressing
⅛ teaspoon dried rosemary leaves,
      crushed, or oregano or marjoram
      leaves
    Salt and pepper

Remove fell (the paperlike covering) if it is on chop. Slash diagonally outer edge of fat on chop at 1-inch intervals to prevent curling (do not cut into lean).

Place chop on rack in broiler pan. Set oven control to broil and/or 550°. Broil with top about 3 inches from heat until brown, about 6 minutes; turn. Brush chop with dressing; sprinkle with rosemary. Broil until done, 5 to 7 minutes. Sprinkle with salt and pepper. Serve with mint jelly if desired.

Broiled Cheese Tomato

1 medium tomato, cut into halves
1 teaspoon margarine or butter
    Seasoned salt
2 tablespoons shredded Monterey Jack or
      Cheddar cheese

Place tomato halves on rack in broiler pan. Dot tomato halves with margarine; sprinkle with seasoned salt. Top with cheese. Set oven control to broil and/or 550°. Broil with tops about 3 inches from heat until tomato is hot and cheese is melted, about 5 minutes.

Zucchini-Pear Salad

1 tablespoon vegetable oil
1½ teaspoons lemon juice
¼ teaspoon sugar
⅛ teaspoon salt
    Dash of pepper
½ small zucchini or cucumber,
      thinly sliced
½ pear or 1 canned pear half, cut into
      ¾-inch pieces
    Salad greens

Mix oil, lemon juice, sugar, salt and pepper; toss with zucchini and pear. Refrigerate at least 1 hour. Remove zucchini and pear with slotted spoon. Serve on salad greens.

Double Grape Tapioca

⅓ cup grape juice*
⅓ cup sweet red wine
2 teaspoons sugar
2 teaspoons quick-cooking tapioca
½ can (5-ounce size) vanilla pudding
      (about ¼ cup)
2 tablespoons half-and-half or milk

Mix grape juice, wine, sugar and tapioca in 1-quart saucepan; let stand 5 minutes. Heat to boiling, stirring occasionally. Remove from heat. Let stand 20 minutes; stir. Spoon into dish; refrigerate until firm, at least 2 hours. Mix pudding and half-and-half until smooth; spoon over tapioca.

*⅔ cup grape juice and 1 teaspoon lemon juice can be substituted for the ⅓ cup grape juice, the wine and sugar.

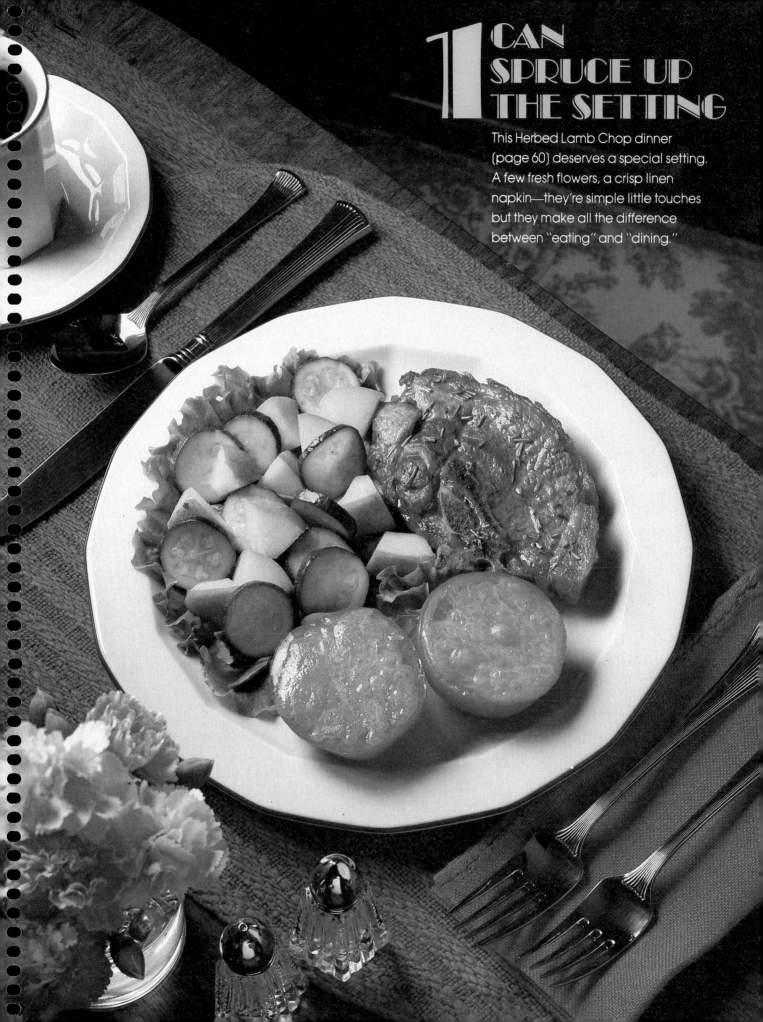

11 CAN SPRUCE UP THE SETTING

This Herbed Lamb Chop dinner (page 60) deserves a special setting. A few fresh flowers, a crisp linen napkin—they're simple little touches but they make all the difference between "eating" and "dining."

Bacon-wrapped Beef Tenderloin

1 slice bacon
1 beef tenderloin fillet, about ¾ inch
    thick (about 4 ounces)
    Salt and pepper
1 slice bread, taosted and cut into fourths

Wrap bacon around edge of beef; secure with wooden pick. Place beef on rack in broiler pan. Set oven control to broil and/or 550°. Broil with top about 3 inches from heat until brown, about 8 minutes. Turn; broil until brown, 4 to 6 minutes. Sprinkle with salt and pepper. Serve on toast points.

Stuffed Mushrooms

6 medium mushrooms (1½ to 2 inches in
    diameter)
2 tablespoons margarine or butter, melted
1 tablespoon grated Parmesan cheese
1 teaspoon snipped parsley

Remove stems from mushroom caps; reserve. Form pan, 7x5 inches, from aluminum foil. Dip mushroom caps into margarine. Place mushroom caps, stem sides up, in foil pan. Reserve remaining margarine. Chop reserved mushroom stems. Mix chopped stems, cheese, parsley and reserved margarine. Spoon mixture into mushroom caps.

Place foil pan on rack in broiler pan. Set oven control to broil and/or 550°. Broil with tops about 3 inches from heat until hot, 4 to 6 minutes.

Blue Cheese Tossed Salad

1 cup bite-size pieces salad greens
¼ cup cauliflowerets
2 to 3 tablespoons Blue Cheese Dressing
    (below)
    Crumbled blue cheese
1 small tomato, cut into wedges

Toss salad greens and cauliflowerets. Spoon dressing over top; sprinkle with blue cheese. Top with tomato wedges.

BLUE CHEESE DRESSING

1 package (3 ounces) cream cheese,
    softened
¼ cup milk
2 tablespoons vegetable oil
¼ teaspoon sugar
¼ teaspoon seasoned salt
¼ cup crumbled blue cheese
    (about 1 ounce)

Beat all ingredients except blue cheese with hand beater or fork until smooth; stir in blue cheese. Cover and store dressing in refrigerator. Stir before using.

English Trifle

2 ladyfingers, cut crosswise into halves
    and separated*
2 teaspoons dry white wine, if desired
½ can (5-ounce size) vanilla pudding
    (about ¼ cup)
1 tablespoon raspberry or strawberry
    jam or preserves
¼ cup frozen whipped topping, thawed
    Sliced almonds

Layer half each of the ladyfinger pieces, wine and pudding in dish; dot with jam. Repeat with remaining ladyfinger pieces, wine and pudding; spread with whipped topping. Sprinkle with almonds. Refrigerate at least 1 hour.

*1 slice pound cake (¾ inch thick), cut into sixths, can be substituted for the ladyfingers.

BEEF STRIPS
BAKED POTATO DELUXE
CAULIFLOWER-CARROT BAKE
ORANGE CREPES

Beef Strips

¼ pound beef boneless sirloin or round
    steak, about ½ inch thick
2 tablespoons vegetable oil
2 tablespooons dry bread crumbs or
    cracker crumbs
⅛ teaspoon onion salt
⅛ teaspoon dry mustard
⅛ teaspoon paprika
1 tablespoon all-purpose flour or
    buttermilk baking mix
1 egg white, slightly beaten

Cut beef into 1-inch strips. Heat oil in baking pan, 8x8x2 inches, in 375° oven until hot, about 5 minutes; remove from oven.

Mix bread crumbs, onion salt, mustard and paprika. Coat beef strips with flour; dip into egg white, then coat with bread crumb mixture. Place in oil in pan. Cook uncovered in 375° oven 10 minutes; turn. Cook until beef is done, about 15 minutes.

Baked Potato Deluxe

1 medium baking potato
1 slice bacon, crisply fried and crumbled
2 tablespoons dairy sour cream or plain
    yogurt
2 teaspoons grated Parmesan cheese
½ teaspoon snipped chives or parsley
    Dash of pepper

Prick potato with fork to allow steam to escape. If desired, rub with shortening for softer skin. Cook in 375° oven until soft, 1 to 1¼ hours.

Mix remaining ingredients. Cut crisscross gash in top of potato; squeeze gently until some potato pops up through opening. Top with sour cream mixture.

Cauliflower-Carrot Bake

½ cup cauliflowerets
1 medium carrot, cut diagonally into
    ½-inch slices
⅛ teaspoon salt
    Ground nutmeg, if desired
1 teaspoon margarine or butter

Place cauliflowerets and carrot in ungreased 10-ounce casserole or custard cup. Sprinkle with salt and nutmeg; dot with margarine. Cover and cook in 375° oven until tender, 25 to 30 minutes.

Orange Crepes

  Crepes (below)*
¼ cup orange marmalade
1 tablespoon margarine or butter
1 tablespoon water
1 tablespoon powdered sugar
1 teaspoon orange-flavored liqueur

Prepare Crepes. Heat marmalade, margarine and water to boiling. Boil and stir 1 minute; remove from heat. Sprinkle each crepe with powdered sugar; fold into fourths. Dip crepes into marmalade mixture. Stir liqueur into remaining marmalade mixture; pour over crepes.

*1 package frozen Freezer Crepes (page 56), thawed, can be substituted for the Crepes.

CREPES

¼ cup all-purpose flour
½ teaspoon sugar
⅛ teaspoon baking powder
⅛ teaspoon salt
⅓ cup milk
1 egg yolk
1 teaspoon vegetable oil

Beat all ingredients with fork until smooth. Lightly butter 7- or 8-inch skillet; heat over medium heat until butter is bubbly. Pour about ¼ cup batter into skillet; rotate skillet until batter covers bottom. Cook until light brown; turn and cook other side until light brown. Repeat with remaining batter. Keep crepes covered.   2 crepes.

Spaghetti-Cheese Toss

3 to 4 ounces uncooked thin spaghetti
2 slices bacon, cut into ½-inch pieces
3 tablespoons dry white wine or dry
    vermouth
1 egg, well beaten
2 tablespoons grated Parmesan or
    Romano cheese
    Freshly ground pepper

Cook spaghetti as directed on package; drain but do not rinse.

Fry bacon over medium heat until almost crisp; remove bacon and drain. Stir wine into hot bacon fat. Heat to boiling. Boil and stir 2 minutes.

Stir spaghetti into wine mixture; add bacon, egg and cheese. Toss over low heat until egg adheres to spaghetti and appears cooked. Sprinkle with pepper and, if desired, additional grated Parmesan or Romano cheese.

Antipasto Vegetable Salad

1 tablespoon bottled Italian dressing
1 cup bite-size pieces salad greens
½ small zucchini, thinly sliced
1 green onion (with top), sliced
2 teaspoons sliced ripe olives
    Seasoned Croutons (page 72)
    Hot cherry pepper

Toss dressing, salad greens, zucchini, onion and olives. Sprinkle with Seasoned Croutons. Top with hot cherry pepper.

Pork Chop and Orange Stuffing

1 smoked pork chop, about ½ inch thick,
   or 1 pork chop, about ½ inch thick
2 tablespoons chopped celery
1 tablespoon chopped onion
2 tablespoons margarine or butter
½ cup seasoned croutons
2 tablespoons coarsely chopped nuts
1 small orange, pared and sectioned

Place chop in ungreased 20-ounce casserole. Cook and stir celery and onion in margarine in 1-quart saucepan over medium heat until onion is tender, about 5 minutes. Toss celery mixture, croutons and nuts; carefully stir in orange sections. Spoon mixture evenly over chop. Cover and cook in 350° oven 30 minutes. Uncover and cook until stuffing is dry on top, 15 to 20 minutes.

Peas in Squash

½ acorn squash
1 tablespoon margarine or butter
   Onion salt
¼ cup frozen green peas

Place squash, cut side up, in ungreased baking pan 8x8x2 inches. Spoon margarine into center of squash. Cook uncovered in 350° oven 45 minutes. Spoon margarine from center of squash over cut edge of squash; sprinkle with onion salt. Place peas in center of squash; cover with aluminum foil. Cook until squash is tender and peas are hot, about 30 minutes.

Ginger Pear Parfait

½ package (3-ounce size) cream cheese,
   softened
1 tablespoon powdered sugar
⅛ teaspoon finely shredded lemon peel
   or orange peel
½ teaspoon lemon juice or orange juice
¼ cup gingersnap crumbs (about 4
   gingersnaps)
2 canned pear or peach halves, cut into
   ½-inch pieces

Beat cream cheese, powdered sugar, lemon peel and lemon juice with hand beater or fork until fluffy. Spoon ⅓ of the gingersnap crumbs into parfait glass. Top with half of the pears and half of the cream cheese mixture; repeat. Sprinkle with remaining crumbs. Refrigerate at least 1 hour.

1 Should Know...

To end up with a glorious dessert, you don't have to start making it hours before. In little more time than it takes to open a can, carton or jar, you can concoct any number of quick and delicious desserts. Consider these ideas:
- Top lemon sherbet with jam or fruit-flavored liqueur.
- Place ½ pint vanilla ice cream and 1 tablespoon grenadine, crème de menthe or brandy in blender container. Cover and blend until smooth.
- Scoop ice cream onto a brownie square and smother with chocolate sauce.
- Fill a split ladyfinger with canned chocolate pudding and drizzle with fudge sauce.
- Add a splash of white wine or ginger ale to a goblet of whole fresh strawberries.
- Sprinkle your favorite fresh or frozen fruits with orange-flavored liqueur or partially thawed frozen fruit juice concentrate.

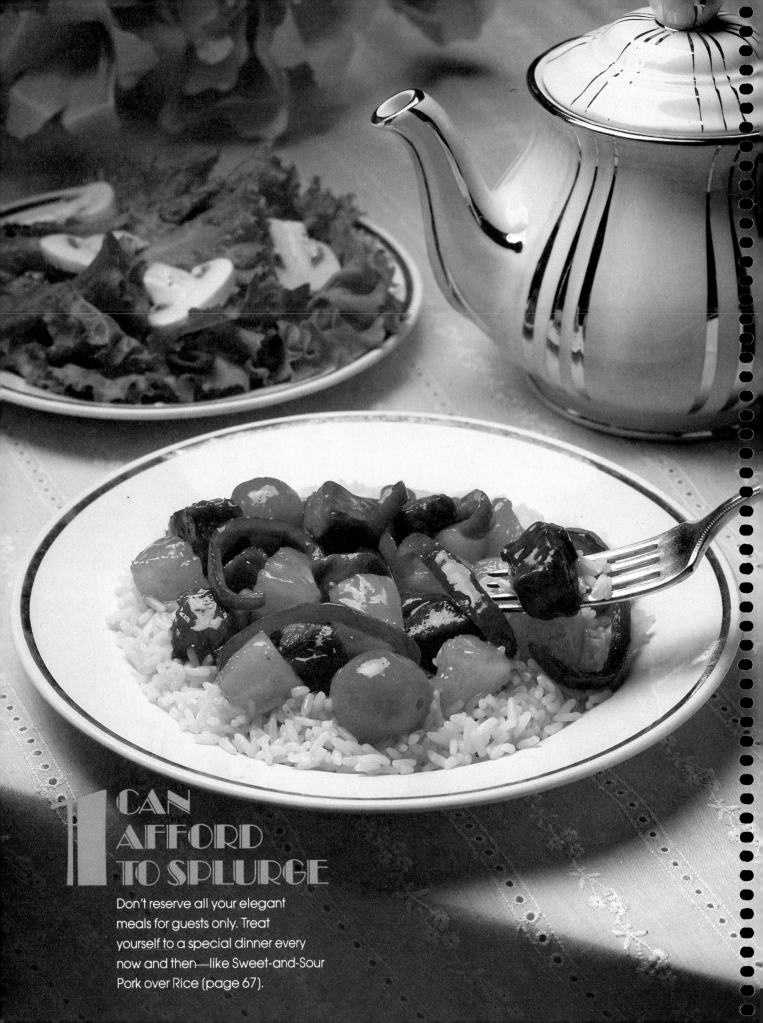

CAN AFFORD TO SPLURGE

Don't reserve all your elegant meals for guests only. Treat yourself to a special dinner every now and then—like Sweet-and-Sour Pork over Rice (page 67).

Sweet-and-Sour Pork over Rice

1 pork tenderloin (about 3 ounces),
    cut into ¾-inch pieces
1 teaspoon vegetable oil
½ can (8¼-ounce size) pineapple chunks
    (about ½ cup drained; reserve ¼ cup
    syrup)
2 tablespoons sugar
2 tablespoons catsup
¼ teaspoon soy sauce
2 drops red pepper sauce
    Quick Rice (right)
1 teaspoon cornstarch
1 tablespoon water
¼ medium green pepper, cut into
    ¼-inch strips
3 cherry tomatoes

Cook and stir pork pieces in oil in 8-inch skillet over medium heat until brown, about 10 minutes. Add enough water to reserved pineapple syrup to measure ⅓ cup. Stir syrup mixture, sugar, catsup, soy sauce and pepper sauce into skillet. Heat to boiling. Reduce heat; cover and simmer until pork is done, 8 to 10 minutes.

Prepare Quick Rice. Mix cornstarch and water; stir into pork mixture. Cook, stirring constantly, until mixture thickens and boils. Boil and stir 1 minute. Stir in pineapple chunks, green pepper and tomatoes; heat until pineapple and tomatoes are hot. Serve over Quick Rice.

QUICK RICE
⅓ cup water
½ teaspoon margarine or butter
⅛ teaspoon salt
⅓ cup uncooked instant rice

Heat water, margarine and salt to boiling in 1-quart saucepan. Stir in rice. Cover; remove from heat. Let stand until rice is tender, about 5 minutes. Stir rice with fork until fluffy.

To Microwave Sweet-and-Sour Pork: Mix pork pieces, reserved ¼ cup pineapple syrup, the sugar, catsup, soy sauce, pepper sauce and cornstarch in ungreased 1-quart microwaveproof casserole. Cover tightly and microwave on high (full) power 2 minutes; stir. Cover tightly and microwave on high (full) power until pork is done, 4 to 5 minutes longer. Stir in pineapple chunks, green pepper and tomatoes. Cover tightly and microwave on high (full) power until pineapple and tomatoes are hot, about 1½ minutes.

To Microwave Quick Rice: Microwave water, margarine and salt uncovered in 1-pint microwaveproof measure to boiling, on high (full) power, 1½ minutes. Stir in rice. Cover tightly and let stand until rice is tender, about 5 minutes. Stir rice with fork until fluffy.

STUFFED HAM ROLLS
CREAMY NOODLES
AVOCADO SALAD
WINE
DINNER MINTS

Stuffed Ham Rolls

4 frozen asparagus spears
⅓ package (6-ounce size) frozen cooked
    crabmeat, cut into two 1-inch sticks
2 thin slices fully cooked smoked ham
2 tablespoons shredded Monterey Jack
    or Swiss cheese

Rinse frozen asparagus under running cold water to separate. Place 1 frozen stick crabmeat and 2 asparagus spears on narrow end of each ham slice; roll up and secure with wooden pick. Place rolls, seam sides down, in ungreased baking pan, 8x8x2 inches, or pie plate, 9x1¼ inches. Cook uncovered in 350° oven 15 minutes. Sprinkle with cheese; cook uncovered until crabmeat is hot and cheese is melted, about 5 minutes.

Note: Use a sharp knife to cut frozen crabmeat. Store remaining frozen crabmeat in sealed package in freezer.

Creamy Noodles

1 cup uncooked noodles
    (about 2 ounces)
¼ cup half-and-half or milk
2 tablespoons mayonnaise or salad
    dressing
1 teaspooon margarine or butter
⅛ teaspoon salt
4 to 6 drops red pepper sauce

Heat 1 quart water and 1 teaspoon salt to boiling in 2-quart saucepan. Add noodles. Boil uncovered, stirring occasionally, just until tender, 7 to 10 minutes; drain. Heat remaining ingredients over low heat, stirring constantly, until smooth and hot. Stir in noodles gently until coated.

Avocado Salad

1 small grapefruit*
½ medium avocado, sliced
    Lettuce leaves
1 tablespoon honey
1 tablespoon chopped macadamia nuts
    or cashews

Pare and section grapefruit; reserve 2 tablespoons juice. Arrange grapefruit and avocado on lettuce leaves. Mix honey and grapefruit juice; drizzle over salad. Sprinkle with nuts.

*1 can (8 ounces) grapefruit sections, drained, and 2 teaspoons light grapefruit syrup can be substituted for the small grapefruit and grapefruit juice.

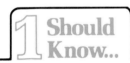 **Should Know...**

A ripe avocado, sliced or chunked, can add a wealth of goodness to a simple salad. And, best of all, avocados can be bought by the avocado! Don't use an avocado until it's ripe (it will yield to gentle pressure), even if it means letting it stand at room temperature a few days. Then cut lengthwise into halves; twist halves and remove pit (use knife to remove if necessary). Sprinkle cut surface of any unused portions with lemon juice; cover and refrigerate. Use as soon as possible.

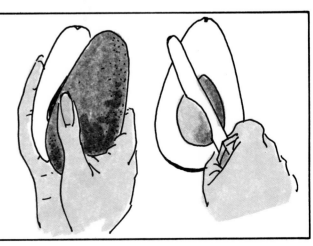

SHRIMP TEMPURA
STEAMED RICE
LEMON SHERBET
ALMOND COOKIES

Shrimp Tempura

Vegetable oil
½ cup buttermilk baking mix
⅓ cup water
1 egg
¼ pound fresh or frozen (thawed)
    shrimp, shelled and deveined
    (about 5)
3 mushrooms, cut into halves
1 carrot, cut into 2x¼-inch strips
½ zucchini, cut into ¼-inch slices
    Lemon-Soy Sauce or Plum Sauce
    (below)

Heat oil (1 inch) to 350°. Beat baking mix, water and egg with hand beater or fork until smooth. Pat shrimp and vegetables dry; dip into batter. Fry several pieces at a time in hot oil, turning once, until golden brown, 2 to 3 minutes; drain. Serve with Lemon-Soy Sauce.

LEMON-SOY SAUCE

2 tablespoons soy sauce
2 tablespoons lemon juice
1 tablespoon dry white wine

Mix all ingredients.

PLUM SAUCE

2 tablespoons chili sauce
2 tablespoons plum or grape jelly
⅛ teaspoon red pepper sauce

Mix all ingredients.

Steamed Rice

3 tablespoons uncooked regular rice
⅓ cup plus 1 tablespoon water
⅛ teaspoon salt

Heat rice, water and salt to boiling in 1-quart saucepan, stirring occasionally. Reduce heat; cover and simmer 14 minutes. (Do not lift cover or stir.) Remove pan from heat. Fluff rice lightly with fork; cover and let steam 5 to 10 minutes.

Almond Cookies

⅔ cup buttermilk baking mix
¼ cup sugar
2 tablespoons shortening
1 egg, separated
¼ teaspoon almond extract
¼ teaspoon vanilla
    About 12 whole blanched almonds

Heat oven to 350°. Mix baking mix, sugar, shortening, egg yolk, almond extract and vanilla. Work mixture with hands until dough holds together. Shape by rounded teaspoonfuls into 1-inch balls. Place about 2 inches apart on ungreased cookie sheet. Flatten each ball to ¼ inch with bottom of greased glass dipped in sugar. Press almond into center of each cookie. Beat egg white slightly; brush on each cookie. Bake until golden brown, about 15 minutes. Cool 1 minute before removing from cookie sheet. About 1 dozen cookies.

PEACHY ROCK CORNISH HEN
ALMOND BROWN RICE
ASPARAGUS
WITH LEMON WEDGE
CHOCOLATE CREAM

Peachy Rock Cornish Hen

1 frozen Rock Cornish hen (¾ to
    1 pound), thawed
    Salt
    Margarine or butter, melted
2 tablespoons peach or orange
    marmalade or jam
½ teaspoon soy sauce
    Dash of garlic powder

Sprinkle cavity of hen with salt. Place hen, breast side up, on rack in shallow roasting pan; brush with margarine. Roast uncovered in 350° oven, brushing with margarine 3 or 4 times, 45 minutes.

Mix remaining ingredients. Brush hen with marmalade mixture. Roast uncovered until hen is done, brushing with marmalade mixture once, about 15 minutes. Cut hen with kitchen scissors, cutting along backbone from tail to neck, into halves. Serve one half immediately.

Note: Wrap remaining half hen in aluminum foil and label; freeze no longer than 1 month. To serve, heat frozen cooked hen in aluminum foil in 350° oven until hot, about 45 minutes. Open aluminum foil; heat uncovered 10 minutes longer.

Almond Brown Rice

¼ cup uncooked brown or regular rice
1 tablespoon sliced almonds
1 tablespoon margarine or butter
½ cup boiling water
1 teaspoon instant chicken bouillon

Cook and stir rice and almonds in margarine over medium heat until almonds are brown, about 3 minutes. Mix rice mixture, water and instant bouillon in ungreased 15- or 16-ounce casserole or custard cup. Cover and cook in 350° oven 30 minutes. Stir with fork; cover and cook until liquid is absorbed, about 10 minutes longer.

Asparagus with Lemon Wedge

½ package (10-ounce size) asparagus
    spears
1 teaspoon margarine or butter
    Salt and pepper
    Lemon wedge

Cook asparagus as directed on package; drain. Toss with margarine; sprinkle with salt and pepper. Serve with lemon wedge.

Note: Use end of knife or fork to separate frozen asparagus spears. Store remaining frozen asparagus spears in sealed package in freezer.

Chocolate Cream

2 bars (1.45 ounces each) dark, mildly
    sweet chocolate candy or 2 bars
    (1.45 ounces each) milk chocolate
    or milk chocolate candy with almonds
1 tablespoon margarine or butter
½ cup frozen whipped topping, thawed

Heat chocolate and margarine over low heat, stirring constantly, until chocolate is melted; remove from heat. Cool slightly; fold into whipped topping. Spoon into dessert dish; refrigerate at least 30 minutes. Top with additional whipped topping and ½ teaspoon brandy if desired.

1 CAN CELEBRATE THE OCCASION

It doesn't really matter what the occasion is. What *does* matter is that you feel good about today — so plan to enjoy it with this Peachy Rock Cornish Hen dinner (page 70).

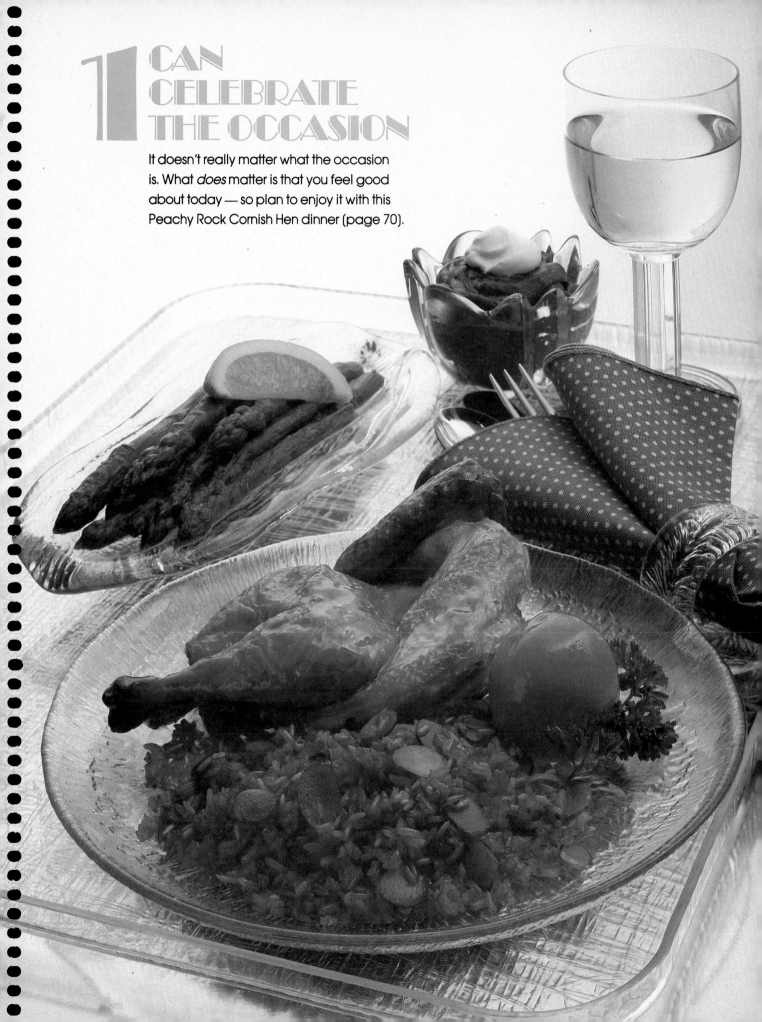

Clam Sauce over Noodles

1 cup uncooked green noodles (about 2 ounces)
1 clove garlic, finely chopped
1 tablespoon margarine or butter
1 can (6½ ounces) minced clams, drained (reserve 2 tablespoons juice)
2 tablespoons dry white wine
1 teaspoon snipped parsley
6 to 8 drops red pepper sauce

Cook noodles as directed on package; drain. Cook and stir garlic in margarine over medium heat until garlic is golden brown. Stir in remaining ingredients. Heat to boiling; pour over noodles.

Tossed Greens and Croutons

Seasoned Croutons (right)
1 tablespoon vegetable oil
2 teaspoons vinegar
1 teaspoon lemon juice
Dash each of salt, dry mustard and paprika
1 cup bite-size pieces salad greens

Prepare Seasoned Croutons. Shake oil, vinegar, lemon juice, salt, mustard and paprika in tightly covered jar; toss with salad greens and ¼ cup of the croutons. Sprinkle with additional croutons if desired.

SEASONED CROUTONS

1 tablespoon margarine or butter
1 slice bread, cut into ½-inch cubes
¼ teaspoon seasoned salt

Heat margarine in baking pan, 8x8x2 inches, in 400° oven until melted. Toss bread cubes and seasoned salt with margarine until cubes are coated. Toast, stirring occasionally, until crisp and golden brown, about 10 minutes.

Cheese Croutons: Substitute 2 teaspoons grated Parmesan cheese for the seasoned salt.

Dill Croutons: Substitute dried dill weed for the seasoned salt.

Garlic Croutons: Substitute ⅛ teaspoon garlic powder and dash of salt for the seasoned salt.

Italian Herb Croutons: Substitute Italian herb seasoning for the seasoned salt.

When One Meal Leads To Another

"I love steak and I love potatoes. But two nights in a row? Boring!"

Sure it can be boring, but it doesn't have to be. With a little planning, that steak-and-potato meal can be reprised as a whole new thing.

Variations on a theme is what this chapter is all about —so think "planovers" not "leftovers." So different are these once-again (and even twice-again) menus, you'll hardly be aware that they share the same shopping list.

That familiar beef steak, for instance, is featured in four quick-switch dinner plans, each with its own compatible accompaniments. Fish fillets, turkey drumstick, chicken breast, veal and liver similarly appear in well-disguised repeat performances. Pudding is used in a parfait one day; mixed with a bit of wine, it's cake topping on another day. Canned corn accents a chilled relish at one meal; combined with zucchini, it's a hot vegetable later in the week.

Using these 15 menus as your guide, learn to plan your meals with return engagements in mind.

A touch of foreign flair! What happens when beef steak goes
Oriental one night and Hungarian another is nothing short of delectable.
And three cheers for the two very distinctive cucumber salads.

SUKIYAKI
STEAMED RICE
SESAME CUCUMBER SALAD
TEA

Sukiyaki

½ pound beef boneless sirloin steak
2 teaspoons vegetable oil
¼ cup water
1 tablespoon soy sauce
1 teaspoon sugar
1 teaspoon instant beef bouillon
2 green onions (with tops), cut into
    1½-inch pieces
1 small carrot, cut diagonally into
    ⅛-inch slices
1 small stalk celery, cut diagonally into
    ⅛-inch slices
4 mushrooms, thinly sliced
1 cup spinach
  Steamed Rice (page 69)

Cut beef across grain into 2x¼-inch strips. Cover and refrigerate half of the beef and use within 2 days for Hungarian Beef (page 76). Cook and stir remaining beef in oil in 8-inch skillet over medium heat until brown. Stir in water, soy sauce, sugar and instant bouillon. Arrange beef in one half of skillet. Arrange onions and carrot in separate sections of skillet. Heat to boiling. Reduce heat; cover and simmer 10 minutes. Arrange celery, mushrooms and spinach in separate sections of skillet. Heat to boiling. Reduce heat; cover and simmer until spinach is cooked, about 5 minutes. Serve with Steamed Rice.

To Microwave: Cover tightly and microwave carrot, celery and 1 tablespoon water in ungreased 1½-quart microwaveproof casserole on high (full) power until crisp-tender, 2 minutes. Remove vegetables with slotted spoon; reserve. Stir beef, soy sauce, sugar, instant bouillon and onions into casserole. Cover loosely and microwave on high (full) power until beef is done, about 2 minutes. Arrange beef and onions in one half of casserole. Arrange carrot, celery, mushrooms and spinach in separate sections of casserole. Cover loosely and microwave on high (full) power until vegetables are done, 2 to 3 minutes.

To Prepare Sukiyaki Only: Cut ¼ pound beef boneless sirloin steak across grain into 2x¼-inch strips. Continue as directed.

Sesame Cucumber Salad

½ medium cucumber, thinly sliced
1 tablespoon vinegar
1 teaspoon sugar
⅛ teaspoon salt
1 teaspoon toasted sesame seed

Mix cucumber, vinegar, sugar and salt in glass bowl. Cover and refrigerate cucumber mixture at least 4 hours.

Remove cucumber from bowl with slotted spoon. Sprinkle with sesame seed.

Note: To toast sesame seed, heat in 6-inch skillet, stirring occasionally, until golden brown.

Cut beef across grain into 2x¼-inch strips. Cover and refrigerate remaining half (see page 76).

Arrange browned beef, onions and carrot in separate sections of skillet.

Hungarian Beef

    Beef strips from Sukiyaki
2   tablespoons chopped onion
½   clove garlic, finely chopped, or dash of
      garlic powder
1   tablespoon vegetable oil
4   mushrooms, sliced
½   cup water
1   tablespoon catsup
1   teaspoon instant beef bouillon
½   teaspoon paprika
¼   teaspoon salt
¼   cup water
1   tablespoon all-purpose flour
¼   cup dairy sour cream
    Buttered Macaroni (below)

Cook and stir beef, onion and garlic in oil in 8-inch skillet over medium heat until beef is brown. Stir in mushrooms, ½ cup water, the catsup, instant bouillon, paprika and salt. Heat to boiling. Reduce heat; cover and simmer until beef is done, about 15 minutes. Mix ¼ cup water and the flour; stir into beef mixture. Heat to boiling, stirring constantly. Boil and stir 1 minute.

Stir in sour cream. Heat, stirring occasionally, until hot. Serve over Buttered Macaroni.

BUTTERED MACARONI

Heat 1 quart water and 1 teaspoon salt to boiling in 2-quart saucepan. Add ⅓ cup uncooked macaroni. Boil uncovered, stirring occasionally, just until tender, 7 to 10 minutes; drain. Toss with 1 teaspoon margarine or butter.

To Microwave Hungarian Beef: Mix beef and oil in ungreased 1-quart microwave-proof casserole. Cover loosely and microwave on high (full) power until beef is done, 2 to 3 minutes. Remove beef from juice in casserole. Stir mushrooms, onion and garlic into casserole. Cover loosely and microwave on high (full) power until onion is tender, about 2 minutes. Stir in catsup, instant bouillon, paprika and salt. Shake water and flour in tightly covered jar; stir into mushroom mixture. Microwave uncovered on high (full) power to boiling, about 30 seconds. Boil until thickened, about 1 minute. Stir in beef and sour cream. Microwave uncovered on high (full) power until hot, about 30 seconds.

To Prepare Hungarian Beef Only: Cut ¼ pound beef boneless sirloin steak across grain into 2x¼-inch strips. Continue as directed.

Cucumber-Lime Mold

3   tablespoons boiling water
¼   package (3-ounce size) lime-flavored
      gelatin (about 1 tablespoon plus
      2 teaspoons)
1   tablespoon mayonnaise or salad
      dressing
½   medium cucumber, shredded and well
      drained
1   teaspoon finely shredded onion
    Spinach leaves

Pour boiling water on gelatin in small bowl; stir until gelatin is dissolved. Stir in mayonnaise with fork until smooth. Refrigerate until slightly thickened but not set, about 20 minutes.

Stir in cucumber and onion; pour into 4-ounce mold or 6-ounce custard cup. Refrigerate until firm, at least 2 hours. Unmold on spinach leaves.

Note: You can prepare individual ½-cup servings of remaining fruit-flavored gelatin. Pour ¼ cup boiling water on about 1 tablespoon plus 1 teaspoon gelatin; stir until gelatin is dissolved. Stir in ¼ cup cold water. Refrigerate until firm, about 3 hours.

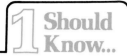

About Coffee and Tea

Whether you choose to serve coffee or tea during or after meals or as a pick-me-up any time during the day, always take the little bit of extra time and effort necessary to prepare a *good* cup of your favorite beverage.

Ground Coffee: Depending on the strength of coffee you prefer, it is generally recommended that for each ¾ cup water, you use 1 level tablespoon coffee for a weak brew, 2 level tablespoons for a medium brew and 3 level tablespoons for a strong brew.

Instant Coffee: Place 1 to 2 teaspoons instant coffee in each cup. Fill with boiling water; stir.

Demitasse: Prepare coffee using ¼ cup ground coffee for each ¾ cup water. Demitasse is served in small cups, often with a twist of lemon peel and sugar.

Iced Coffee: Prepare strong coffee (see above). Fill tall glass with crushed ice. Pour hot coffee over ice. Serve with sugar and cream or whipped cream if desired. Or prepare medium coffee (see above); cool. Pour into ice cube trays; freeze. Pour freshly brewed medium coffee over coffee cubes in tall glasses.

California Coffee: Pour 2 tablespoons brandy into mug. Fill ⅔ full with hot strong coffee (see above). Top with 1 scoop (about ¼ cup) chocolate ice cream.

Dessert Coffee Mix: Place ¼ cup freeze-dried coffee, ½ cup sugar and ½ cup cocoa in blender container. Cover and blend on high speed 15 seconds; stir. Cover and blend on high speed 15 seconds longer. Store in tightly covered container. For each serving, place 2 teaspoons mix in cup. Fill with boiling water. About 1 cup mix.

Cardamon Coffee Mix: Omit cocoa from Dessert Coffee Mix (left). Add ½ teaspoon ground cardamom and ¼ teaspoon ground mace to ingredients in blender container.

Spiced Coffee Mix: Omit cocoa from Dessert Coffee Mix (left). Add ¼ teaspoon ground cinnamon, ¼ teaspoon ground nutmeg and ¼ teaspoon ground allspice to ingredients in blender container.

Tea: Loose tea and tea bags are prepared in the same manner. Start with a glass, china or earthenware teapot. Add boiling water; allow to stand a few minutes then pour out. Heat cold water to a full rolling boil. Add tea or bags to the warm pot (1 teaspoon of loose tea or 1 tea bag for each cup). Pour boiling water over the tea (¾ cup for each cup of tea); let stand 3 to 5 minutes to bring out the flavor. Strain the tea or remove the tea bag. Serve with sugar and milk or lemon if desired.

Spiced Orange Tea: Place 1 teaspoon loose tea, 1 or 2 whole cloves (broken into pieces), ⅛ teaspoon dried orange peel and a dash of ground cinnamon in a heatproof container. Add 1 cup boiling water. Cover and let stand until desired strength, 3 to 5 minutes. Strain.

Iced Tea: Prepare tea as directed (see above) except—double the amount of tea. Strain tea over ice in pitcher or into ice-filled glass. Note: Tea that has been steeped too long or refrigerated will become cloudy. Pour a small amount of boiling water into tea to make it clear again.

Do-Ahead Iced Tea: Use 2 teaspoons loose tea or 2 tea bags for each cup of cold water. Place tea in glass container; add water. Cover and refrigerate at least 24 hours. Serve over crushed ice.

Two good menus with the bonus benefit of cooking only once.
You can score this double play by teaming steak and Brussels sprouts in
two unexpected combinations. Do the same with yogurt and cantaloupe.

MUSTARD STEAK
POTATO WEDGES
BUTTERED BRUSSELS SPROUTS
SUMMER FRUIT BOWL

Mustard Steak

½ pound beef boneless sirloin steak,
    ½ inch thick, cut into halves
    Salt and pepper
1 teaspoon margarine or butter, softened
¼ teaspoon snipped parsley
¼ teaspoon prepared mustard
    Dash of onion salt

Place steak halves on rack in broiler pan. Set oven control to broil and/or 550°. Broil with tops about 3 inches from heat until brown, about 5 minutes; sprinkle with salt and pepper. Turn; broil until done, about 5 minutes. Sprinkle with salt and pepper. Cover and refrigerate 1 steak and use within 2 days for Marinated Beef and Vegetables (page 79). Mix remaining ingredients; spread over remaining steak.

To Prepare Mustard Steak Only: Prepare ¼ pound beef boneless sirloin steak, ½ inch thick, as directed.

Potato Wedges

1 medium potato, cut lengthwise into
    eighths
    Vegetable oil
    Seasoned salt

Place potato wedges on rack in broiler pan. Brush with oil; sprinkle with seasoned salt. Set oven control to broil and/or 550°. Broil with tops about 3 inches from heat until brown, about 5 minutes. Turn; brush with oil. Sprinkle with seasoned salt. Broil until brown and fork-tender, about 5 minutes.

Buttered Brussels Sprouts

1 package (10 ounces) frozen Brussels
    sprouts
1 teaspoon margarine or butter
    Salt and pepper

Cook Brussels sprouts as directed on package; drain. Cover and refrigerate half of the sprouts (about ¾ cup) for Marinated Beef and Vegetables (page 79). Toss remaining sprouts with margarine; sprinkle with salt and pepper.

To Prepare Buttered Brussels Sprouts Only: Divide 1 package (10 ounces) frozen Brussels sprouts into halves. Cook 1 half as directed. Store remaining half in sealed package in freezer.

Summer Fruit Bowl

¼ small cantaloupe, cut into ¾-inch
    pieces (about ¾ cup)
¼ cup blueberries
¼ cup lemon-flavored yogurt
1 tablespoon powdered sugar

Toss all ingredients. Cover and refrigerate remaining cantaloupe and yogurt for Cantaloupe Drink recipe (page 79).

MARINATED BEEF AND VEGETABLES
CORNMEAL MUFFINS
CANTALOUPE DRINK

Marinated Beef and Vegetables

Cooked beef steak from Mustard Steak
Cooked Brussels sprouts from Buttered
    Brussels Sprouts
2 medium mushrooms, sliced
3 thin green pepper rings
3 tablespoons red wine vinegar
1 tablespoon vegetable oil
⅛ teaspoon salt
    Dash each of onion salt, pepper, garlic
      powder and dried tarragon leaves
    Few drops Worcestershire sauce
    Salad greens
3 tomato wedges

Cut beef into ⅜-inch strips. Place beef, Brussels sprouts, mushrooms and green pepper rings in ungreased pie plate, 9x1¼ inches, or shallow glass dish. Mix vinegar, oil, salt, onion salt, pepper, garlic powder, tarragon and Worcestershire sauce; pour over beef and vegetables. Cover and refrigerate, spooning mixture over beef and vegetables occasionally, at least 3 hours.

Spoon beef and vegetables onto salad greens; garnish with tomato wedges.

Cornmeal Muffins

1 egg yolk
¼ cup milk
2 teaspoons vegetable oil
¼ cup buttermilk baking mix
¼ cup yellow or white cornmeal
1 tablespoon sugar

Heat oven to 400°. Grease bottoms of two 6-ounce custard cups. Mix egg yolk, milk and oil. Stir in remaining ingredients; beat vigorously 30 seconds. Divide evenly between custard cups. Bake until golden brown, about 20 minutes.   2 muffins.

Cantaloupe Drink

¼ small cantaloupe from Summer Fruit
    Bowl, cut into ¾-inch pieces
¼ cup lemon-flavored yogurt from
    Summer Fruit Bowl
¼ cup orange juice
1 teaspoon honey
4 ice cubes, crushed (about ½ cup)

Place all ingredients in blender container. Cover and blend on high speed until smooth, 10 seconds. Garnish with orange slice if desired.

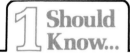

1 Should Know...

Fresh mushrooms will keep fresh up to 4 days if properly stored. Spread in shallow pan; cover loosely and refrigerate. Before using, take just the number you'll need; rinse quickly under cool water and pat dry. Never soak or peel. Trim off stem ends and slice, chop or use whole according to your recipe. When buying, seek out mushrooms with closed or only slightly open caps. Color depends on variety: white, creamy or tan.

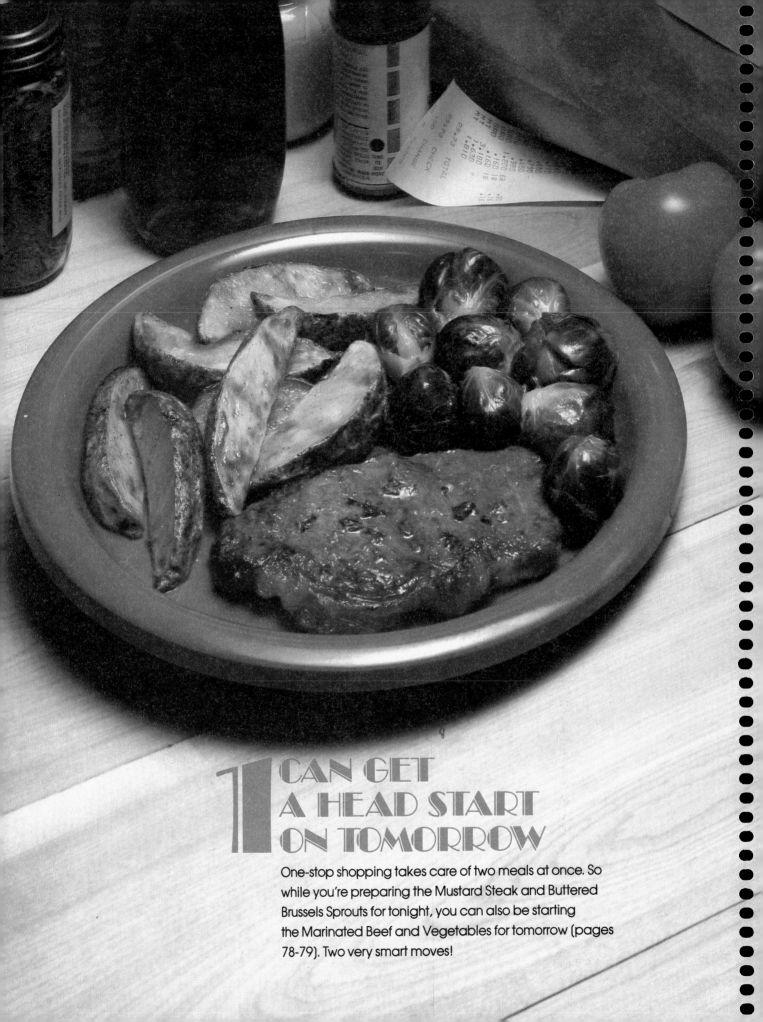

1 CAN GET A HEAD START ON TOMORROW

One-stop shopping takes care of two meals at once. So while you're preparing the Mustard Steak and Buttered Brussels Sprouts for tonight, you can also be starting the Marinated Beef and Vegetables for tomorrow (pages 78-79). Two very smart moves!

No "instant replays" here! Take beef liver, rice, broccoli
and apples. Enjoy them two days in a row, but in decidedly different ways.
An ingenious mix-and-match style of cooking—especially suited to one.

**LIVER WITH APPLES
AND ONIONS
BUTTERED BROCCOLI SPEARS
CURRIED RICE
CHOCOLATE ICE CREAM**

Liver with Apples and Onions

1 tablespoon margarine or butter
3 onion slices, each about ¼ inch thick,
    separated into rings
1 medium apple, cored and cut into
    1-inch rings
1 tablespoon margarine or butter
2 tablespoons all-purpose flour
½ teaspoon salt
⅛ teaspoon pepper
2 pieces beef liver, ⅜ to ½ inch thick
    (about 5 ounces)
½ teaspoon sugar

Heat 1 tablespoon margarine in 8-inch skillet until melted. Arrange onions and apple rings in skillet. Cook over medium heat, stirring onions occasionally and turning apple rings, until tender, about 4 minutes. Remove onions and apple rings; reserve.

Heat 1 tablespoon margarine in skillet until melted. Mix flour, salt and pepper; coat liver with flour mixture. Cook liver in margarine over medium heat, turning once, until done, 4 to 6 minutes. Cover and refrigerate 1 piece liver and use within 2 days for Liver Creole (page 83). Arrange onions and apple rings in skillet with liver. Sprinkle sugar over apple rings. Cover and cook 3 minutes.

To Prepare Liver with Apples and Onions Only: Prepare as directed except—mix 1 tablespoon flour, ¼ teaspoon salt and dash of pepper. Coat 1 piece liver, ⅜ to ½ inch thick (about 2½ ounces), with flour mixture. Continue as directed.

Buttered Broccoli Spears

1 package (10 ounces) frozen broccoli
    spears
1 teaspoon margarine or butter
    Salt and pepper

Cook broccoli as directed on package; drain. Cover and refrigerate half of the spears for Broccoli with Sour Cream (page 83). Toss remaining spears with margarine; sprinkle with salt and pepper.

Curried Rice

⅔ cup water
⅓ cup uncooked regular rice
¼ teaspoon salt
1 tablespoon raisins
1 teaspoon margarine or butter
⅛ teaspoon curry powder
    Dash of onion salt

Heat water, rice and salt to boiling, stirring occasionally. Reduce heat; cover and simmer 14 minutes. (Do not lift cover or stir.) Remove pan from heat. Fluff rice lightly with fork; cover and let steam 5 to 10 minutes. Divide rice into halves (about ½ cup each). Cover and refrigerate one half for Liver Creole (page 83). Toss remaining rice with raisins, margarine, curry powder and onion salt.

To Prepare Curried Rice Only: Heat ¼ cup plus 2 tablespoons water, 3 tablespoons uncooked rice and ⅛ teaspoon salt to boiling, stirring once. Continue as directed except—do not divide rice into halves.

Liver Creole

1 slice bacon, cut into ½-inch pieces
2 tablespoons chopped onion
   Cooked beef liver from Liver with
      Apples and Onions, cut into
      1½x¼-inch strips
½ can (8-ounce size) stewed tomatoes
      (about ½ cup)
   Cooked regular rice from Curried Rice

Fry bacon in 8-inch skillet until crisp; drain and reserve. Cook and stir onion and liver in bacon fat over medium heat until onion is tender, about 3 minutes; stir in tomatoes and rice. Heat, stirring occasionally, until hot, about 3 minutes. Sprinkle with reserved bacon.

To Prepare Liver Creole Only: Mix 1 tablespoon flour, ¼ teaspoon salt and dash of pepper. Coat 1 piece liver, ⅜ to ½ inch thick (about 2½ ounces), with flour mixture. Heat 1 tablespoon margarine or butter over medium heat until melted. Cook liver in margarine, turning once, until done, 4 to 6 minutes. Cool; cut into 1½x¼-inch strips. Continue as directed.

Broccoli with Sour Cream

   Cooked broccoli spears from Buttered
      Broccoli Spears
1 tablespoon bottled Italian dressing
1 teaspoon dairy sour cream or plain
      yogurt

Cut broccoli into pieces. Mix broccoli pieces with dressing. Cover and refrigerate, stirring occasionally, at least 3 hours. Top with sour cream.

Apple Crisp

1 small cooking apple, pared and sliced
1 tablespoon packed brown sugar
1 tablespoon all-purpose flour
1 tablespoon oats
   Dash each of ground cinnamon,
      ground nutmeg and salt
1 tablespoon margarine or butter,
      softened

Place apple slices in ungreased 10-ounce casserole or custard cup. Mix remaining ingredients; sprinkle over apple slices. Cook uncovered in 375° oven until apple slices are tender and topping is golden brown, about 20 minutes. Serve warm with half-and-half or ice cream if desired.

Should Know...

For a single serving (1 cup) of regular cooked rice, you need ⅓ cup uncooked rice, ⅔ cup water and ¼ teaspoon salt. If you prefer instant rice, use ½ cup uncooked rice, ½ cup water and ¼ teaspoon salt.

To change the flavor and/or color of plain rice, vary the cooking liquid. Use apple, orange, pineapple or tomato juice for half of the water. Or use chicken or beef broth or bouillon instead of water.

Cooked rice can be stored in the refrigerator for 4 to 5 days. Cover tightly to prevent drying out. To freeze rice, store in a covered container up to 6 months. To reheat cooked rice, place in top of a double boiler over hot water until rice is hot and fluffy, about 10 minutes.

A super shopping strategy: Buy enough veal to serve once hot
with sauce, then chilled as a salad. Mushrooms, salad greens and bananas take
double dinner turns. And vanilla pudding makes two novel desserts.

VEAL IN MUSHROOM SAUCE
BUTTERED NOODLES
TOMATO-OLIVE SALAD
BANANA PUDDING PARFAIT

Veal in Mushroom Sauce

½ pound veal round steak, ½ inch thick,
　　cut into 2x½-inch strips
1 tablespoon margarine or butter
¼ cup frozen green peas
4 mushrooms, sliced
1 tablespoon chopped onion
　　Dash each of salt, pepper and dried
　　　thyme leaves
1 can (7½ ounces) semi-condensed
　　cream of mushroom soup
　　Buttered Noodles (below)

Cook veal in margarine in 8-inch skillet over
medium heat, stirring occasionally, until no
longer pink, about 5 minutes. Cover and
refrigerate half of the veal and use within 2
days for Chilled Veal and Fruit Salad (page
85). Stir peas, mushrooms, onion, salt, pepper, thyme and soup into remaining veal in
skillet. Heat to boiling. Reduce heat; cover
and simmer, stirring occasionally, until veal
is done, about 20 minutes. Serve over Buttered Noodles.

BUTTERED NOODLES

Heat 1 quart water and 1 teaspoon salt to
boiling in 2-quart saucepan. Add ⅔ cup uncooked noodles. Boil uncovered, stirring
occasionally, just until tender, 7 to 10 minutes; drain. Toss with 1 teaspoon margarine
or butter.

To Prepare Veal in Mushroom Sauce Only:
Cut ¼ pound veal round steak, ½ inch thick,
into ¼-inch strips. Continue as directed.

Tomato-Olive Salad

　Oil-Lemon Dressing (below)
3 tomato slices
4 pitted ripe olives
　Lettuce leaves

Prepare Oil-Lemon Dressing; pour over tomatoes and olives. Cover and refrigerate until chilled, at least 3 hours.

Place tomatoes and olives on lettuce leaves;
spoon dressing over top.

OIL-LEMON DRESSING

1 tablespoon vegetable oil
1½ teaspoons lemon juice
1 teaspoon snipped parsley
　Dash each of salt and pepper

Shake all ingredients in tightly covered jar.

Banana Pudding Parfait

½ package (3½-ounce size) vanilla
　　pudding and pie filling (about ¼ cup
　　plus 1 tablespoon)
1 cup milk
1 small banana or ½ medium banana,
　　sliced
　　Whipped topping

Cook and stir pudding mix and milk just to
boiling over medium heat. Remove from
heat. Divide into halves (about ½ cup each).
Press plastic wrap on top of half of the pudding and refrigerate for Cake with Vanilla
Sauce (page 85). Layer remaining pudding
and banana slices in parfait glass or dish.
Top with whipped topping.

To Prepare Banana Pudding Parfait Only:
Use 1 can (5 ounces) vanilla pudding or ½
cup cooked vanilla pudding. Continue as
directed.

Zesty Tomato Juice

1 can (6 ounces) tomato juice, chilled
¼ teaspoon lemon juice
   Dash of Worcestershire sauce
   Dash each of onion salt and dried dill
     weed

Mix all ingredients. Garnish with lemon slice and celery stick if desired.

Chilled Veal and Fruit Salad

   Cooked veal strips from Veal in
     Mushroom Sauce
½ cup Tokay grape halves, seeded
¼ medium green pepper, cut into strips
1 teaspoon lemon juice
⅛ teaspoon salt
1 small banana or ½ medium banana
1 tablespoon mayonnaise or salad
     dressing
1 tablespoon milk or water
1 cup bite-size pieces salad greens
1 tablespoon chopped pecans

Mix veal, grapes, green pepper, lemon juice and salt. Cover and refrigerate at least 2 hours.

Mash half of banana; stir in mayonnaise and milk. Slice remaining half banana; add to veal mixture. Toss veal mixture with banana-mayonnaise mixture. Serve on salad greens; sprinkle with pecans.

To Prepare Chilled Veal and Fruit Salad Only: Cut ¼ pound veal round steak, ½ inch thick, into ¼-inch strips. Cook in 1 tablespoon margarine or butter in 8-inch skillet over medium heat, stirring occasionally, until no longer pink, about 5 minutes; cool. Continue as directed.

Cake with Vanilla Sauce

1 slice pound cake
   Cooked vanilla pudding from
     Banana Pudding Parfait
1 teaspoon dry white wine
   Toasted coconut or coconut

Place cake slice on small cookie sheet or aluminum foil. Set oven control to broil and/or 550°. Broil with top about 3 inches from heat until golden brown, about 2 minutes. Turn; broil until golden brown, about 2 minutes. Mix pudding and wine; spoon onto cake. Sprinkle with coconut.

I Should Know...

Taking full advantage of your freezer means using it for leftover "bits and pieces" as well as those meant-for-the-freezer items. A handy trick is to pack leftovers in individual plastic freezer bags. Then put the bags in one container for ease in finding. Extra nuts or coconut? These stay fresh in the freezer, too, for the next time they are needed. Fresh herbs—washed, drained and wrapped in foil or a plastic bag—will retain flavor (but not texture) when stored in the freezer. And don't toss that other half of the onion. Peel, rinse, chop, then place in boiling water 1½ minutes. Place in ice water, drain and package. Freeze solo servings of bread, rolls, coffee cake and even buttered French bread slices. It is important to remember, particularly with tiny packets, to label the contents, amount and date on each. A strip of masking tape and a marking pen will do the job.

One thought that makes two menus: Plan for tomorrow when
you poach fish and cook potatoes today—and another dinner is well under way.
Green peas and fruit also play important parts in this double feature.

**POACHED FISH
PARSLEYED NEW POTATOES
TANGY DILLED PEAS
FRUIT AND CHEESE**

Poached Fish

1 onion slice
2 lemon slices
1 parsley sprig
1 teaspoon salt
¼ teaspoon pepper
2 fish fillets (about 3 ounces each)
　 Seasoned salt
　 Lemon wedge or slice

Heat 1 inch water, the onion, lemon slices, parsley, salt and pepper to boiling in 8-inch skillet. Place fish in single layer in skillet. Reduce heat; cover and simmer until fish flakes easily with fork, 2 to 3 minutes. Remove fish with slotted spoon. Sprinkle with seasoned salt. Cover and refrigerate 1 fish fillet and use within 3 days for Fish and Vegetable Medley (page 87). Serve remaining fish fillet with lemon wedge.

To Prepare Poached Fish Only: Prepare 1 fish fillet (about 3 ounces) as directed.

Parsleyed New Potatoes

5 small new potatoes (about 10 ounces)
1 tablespoon margarine or butter
1 tablespoon snipped parsley
　 Salt and pepper

Pare a narrow strip around center of each potato. Heat 1 inch salted water (1 teaspoon salt to 1 cup water) to boiling; add potatoes. Cover; heat to boiling. Cook until tender, 20 to 25 minutes; drain. Cover and refrigerate

2 potatoes for Potato Salad (page 87). Toss remaining cooked potatoes with margarine; sprinkle with parsley, salt and pepper.

To Prepare Parsleyed New Potatoes Only: Prepare 3 small new potatoes (about 6 ounces) as directed.

Tangy Dilled Peas

½ cup frozen green peas
1 tablespoon mayonnaise or salad
　 dressing
1 tablespoon milk or water
⅛ teaspoon salt
　 Dash of dried dill weed

Cook peas as directed on package; drain. Mix peas and remaining ingredients in same pan. Heat over low heat just until hot. Store remaining frozen peas in sealed package in freezer.

Fruit and Cheese

Select 1 of the following fruit and cheese combinations; serve with crackers if desired.

1 wedge cantaloupe or melon, ½ cup strawberries and 1 wedge Camembert or Brie cheese (about 1 ounce).

½ apple, 1 small bunch Tokay grapes and 1 wedge Gruyère, Swiss or Cheddar cheese (about 1 ounce).

½ banana, ½ cup dark sweet cherries and 1 wedge Gourmandise or Liederkranz cheese (about 1 ounce).

½ pear, 1 small bunch seedless green grapes and 1 wedge Gouda or Edam cheese (about 1 ounce).

Fish and Vegetable Medley

     Cooked fish fillet from Poached Fish
½ cup frozen green peas
2 radishes, sliced
     Salt and pepper
2 tablespoons bottled Italian dressing
     Lettuce leaves

Place fish in ungreased pie plate, 9x1¼ inches, or shallow glass dish. Arrange peas and radishes on fish; sprinkle with salt and pepper. Drizzle dressing over vegetables. Cover and refrigerate at least 4 hours. Place fish and vegetables on lettuce leaves.

To Prepare Fish and Vegetable Medley Only: Prepare 1 fish fillet (about 3 ounces) as directed in recipe for Poached Fish. Continue as directed.

Potato Salad

1 hard-cooked egg
     Cooked potatoes from Parsleyed New
          Potatoes, diced (about ½ cup)
2 tablespoons chopped celery
2 green onions (with tops), sliced
¼ teaspoon salt
     Dash of pepper
2 tablespoons mayonnaise or salad
          dressing
1 teaspoon prepared mustard

Cut egg crosswise into halves. Slice one half; wrap and refrigerate. Chop remaining half. Mix chopped egg, potatoes, celery, onions, salt and pepper. Toss with mayonnaise and mustard until vegetables are coated. Cover and refrigerate at least 3 hours. Garnish with reserved egg slices.

To Prepare Potato Salad Only: Prepare 2 small new potatoes as directed in recipe for Parsleyed New Potatoes. Continue as directed.

Berry Shortcake

½ cup blueberries, raspberries or sliced
          strawberries
1 tablespoon granulated sugar
⅓ cup buttermilk baking mix
1 tablespoon milk
½ teaspoon granulated sugar
½ teaspoon margarine or butter, softened
1 teaspoon margarine or butter, softened
1 teaspoon packed brown sugar
1 tablespoon chopped almonds
     Whipped topping

Toss berries with 1 tablespoon granulated sugar. Refrigerate at least 1 hour.

Heat oven to 425°. Stir baking mix, milk, ½ teaspoon granulated sugar and ½ teaspoon margarine until soft dough forms. Press dough evenly in bottom of ungreased 10-ounce custard cup or casserole. Spread 1 teaspoon margarine over dough; sprinkle with brown sugar and almonds. Bake until golden brown, about 15 minutes. Spoon sweetened berries over shortcake. Top with dollop of whipped topping; garnish with whole berry if desired.

CAN BE
TWICE
BLESSED

Don't forget to count on double-duty
side dishes and desserts. One cucumber
equals Sesame Cucumber Salad (page 74)
and Cucumber-Lime Mold (page 76). And
a cantaloupe plus yogurt equals Summer
Fruit Bowl (page 78) and Cantaloupe
Drink (page 79).

One run, two hits, no errors! Here's the way to play:
Start this double-header with sautéed chicken in today's line up.
Then bring on a change-of-pace salad as tomorrow's winner.

SAUTÉED CHICKEN BREAST
MARINATED TOMATO SLICES
CUCUMBER SPEARS
DINNER ROLL
ORANGE SLICES IN SYRUP

Sautéed Chicken Breast

1 small whole chicken breast, boned,
   skinned and cut into halves
1 tablespoon margarine or butter
1½ teaspoons vegetable oil
   Salt and pepper
   Paprika
   Snipped parsley

Cook chicken in margarine and oil in 8-inch skillet over medium heat until done, about 4 minutes on each side. Cover and refrigerate 1 chicken breast half and use within 2 days for Chicken-Tomato-Bulgur Salad (page 91). Sprinkle remaining chicken with salt, pepper and paprika. Top with snipped parsley.

To Prepare Sautéed Chicken Breast Only:
Use 1 small chicken breast half, boned and skinned. Continue as directed.

Marinated Tomato Slices

1 medium tomato, cut into 6 slices
2 tablespoons vinegar
1 tablespoon plus 1 teaspoon vegetable
   oil
¼ teaspoon instant minced onion
⅛ teaspoon sugar
1 drop red pepper sauce
1 small clove garlic, crushed

Place tomato slices in small glass or plastic bowl. Mix remaining ingredients; pour over tomato. Cover and refrigerate at least 1 hour. Reserve 3 tomato slices and 1 tablespoon marinade and use within 2 days for Chicken-Tomato-Bulgur Salad (page 91).

To Prepare Marinated Tomato Slices Only:
Use 1 small tomato; cut into 4 slices. Continue as directed.

Orange Slices in Syrup

1 large seedless orange
2 tablespoons sugar
1 tablespoon water
1 teaspoon light corn syrup
1 teaspoon orange-flavored liqueur or
   1 drop orange extract

Cut a few slivers of peel from orange with vegetable parer or sharp knife, being careful not to cut into white membrane; reserve peel. Pare orange, cutting only deep enough to remove all of the white membrane. Cut orange into ¼-inch slices.

Heat sugar, water, corn syrup and reserved orange peel to boiling. Boil, stirring occasionally, 1 minute; remove from heat. Stir in liqueur. Pour mixture over orange slices. Cover and refrigerate at least 1 hour.

CHICKEN-TOMATO-BULGUR SALAD
QUICK CRESCENT ROLLS
CARROT STICKS
CHOCOLATE-DIPPED FRUIT

Chicken-Tomato-Bulgur Salad

½ cup boiling water
¼ cup bulgur (cracked wheat)
  Cooked chicken from Sautéed Chicken
    Breast, cut up
3 slices tomato from Marinated Tomato
    Slices, coarsely chopped
1 tablespoon snipped parsley
1 tablespoon marinade from Marinated
    Tomato Slices
1 tablespoon olive or vegetable oil
½ teaspoon lemon juice
¼ teaspoon pepper
  Dash of coarsely cracked pepper

Pour boiling water over bulgur. Let stand 1 hour; drain. Mix with remaining ingredients. Cover and refrigerate until chilled, about 2 hours. Serve on lettuce leaves if desired.

Quick Crescent Rolls

½ cup buttermilk baking mix
2 tablespoons water
1 tablespoon margarine or butter, melted

Heat oven to 425°. Mix baking mix and water with fork until soft dough forms. Gently smooth dough into a ball on cloth-covered board floured with baking mix. Knead 5 times. Roll dough into rectangle, 7x6 inches; brush with margarine. Cut rectangle diagonally into halves, forming 2 triangles; roll up. Place rolls, with points underneath, on ungreased cookie sheet; curve ends slightly. Brush with margarine. Bake until light brown, 10 to 12 minutes.   2 rolls.

Chocolate-dipped Fruit

¼ cup semisweet chocolate chips
1 teaspoon shortening
3 large strawberries
2 to 3 small clusters seedless grapes

Heat chocolate chips and shortening over low heat, stirring constantly, until smooth; remove from heat. Coat fruit with chocolate mixture, leaving a small portion of fruit uncoated if desired. Place on waxed paper-lined plate. Refrigerate until chocolate is firm, about 30 minutes.

I Should Know...

Bulgur (also called parboiled wheat or wheat pilaf) is whole wheat that has been cooked, dried, partly debranned and cracked into coarse, angular fragments. It is similar to whole wheat in nutritive properties (containing B vitamins and some protein), and resembles brown rice in its chewiness and flavor. Bulgar is one of the basic foods of the Middle East where it is served as an accompaniment to chicken and lamb. It is also used in soups, stews and casseroles and as an alternate for rice. A tasty salad is made with bulgur, black olives, mint and cumin.

Use one part bulgur to two parts liquid—water, tomato juice or broth—depending on the flavor you wish to add.

Divide and conquer. One turkey drumstick provides the "meat" for three winning main dishes. Who'd ever guess you could go so far on just one leg? And sharing the dinner honors twice are gravy, zucchini and corn.

TURKEY POT ROAST
OLD-FASHIONED CORN RELISH
DINNER ROLL
CHOCOLATE-PEANUT BUTTER SUNDAE

Turkey Pot Roast

1 frozen turkey drumstick, thawed
    (about 1½ pounds)
1 tablespoon vegetable oil
1 envelope individual serving instant
    onion soup
1 cup hot water
1 medium potato, cut into fourths
1 small onion, cut into halves
½ medium zucchini, cut lengthwise into
    fourths
    Turkey Onion Gravy (right)

Cook turkey in oil in 10-inch skillet over medium heat until brown. Mix instant soup and water; pour over turkey. Heat to boiling. Reduce heat; cover tightly and simmer on top of range or in 325° oven until tender, 2 to 2½ hours.

About 30 minutes before end of cooking, add potato and onion. About 10 minutes before end of cooking, add zucchini. Cover and refrigerate remaining zucchini for Corny Zucchini Combo (page 93). Cut 3 slices turkey from drumstick (about 2½ ounces). Cover and refrigerate remaining turkey drumstick and use within 2 days for Turkey and Stuffing Casserole (page 93) and Turkish Turkey (page 94). Place turkey slices and vegetables on warm plate, reserving drippings in skillet. Prepare Turkey Onion Gravy; serve with turkey slices and vegetables.

TURKEY ONION GRAVY

Add enough water to reserved drippings to measure 1 cup. Return to skillet. Shake ¼ cup cold water and 2 tablespoons flour in tightly covered jar. Stir flour mixture slowly into dripping mixture in skillet. Heat to boiling, stirring constantly. Boil and stir 1 minute. Sprinkle with salt and pepper. Cover and refrigerate ⅓ cup of the gravy for Turkey and Stuffing Casserole (page 93).

Old-fashioned Corn Relish

2 tablespoons sugar
2 tablespoons vinegar
⅛ teaspoon salt
⅛ teaspoon celery seed
4 drops red pepper sauce
½ can (8-ounce size) whole kernel corn
    (about ⅓ cup drained)
1 tablespoon chopped pimiento
1 tablespoon chopped green pepper

Heat sugar, vinegar, salt, celery seed and pepper sauce to boiling in 1-quart saucepan. Boil and stir 1 minute. Remove from heat; stir in corn. Cover and refrigerate remaining corn for Corny Zucchini Combo (page 93). Stir pimiento and green pepper into corn mixture. Cover and refrigerate at least 4 hours. Serve on lettuce leaves if desired.

Chocolate-Peanut Butter Sundae

1 tablespoon peanut butter
2 tablespoons chocolate-flavored syrup
1 scoop ice cream

Mix peanut butter and syrup. Spoon over ice cream.

Turkey and Stuffing Casserole

1 tablespoon chopped green pepper
1 tablespoon chopped onion
1 tablespoon margarine or butter
1 cup herb-seasoned croutons
2 tablespoons hot water
⅓ cup cut-up cooked turkey from
   Turkey Pot Roast
⅓ cup turkey gravy from Turkey Onion
   Gravy
1 tablespoon cashew pieces or slivered
   almonds

Cook and stir green pepper and onion in margarine in 1-quart saucepan over medium heat until onion is tender, about 3 minutes. Toss with croutons and water. Remove from saucepan; reserve.

Heat turkey and gravy over medium heat until hot and bubbly. Pour turkey mixture into ungreased 10-ounce casserole or custard cup. Spoon crouton mixture over turkey mixture; sprinkle with cashew pieces. Cook uncovered in 350° oven until bubbly and golden brown, 20 to 25 minutes.

Chicken and Stuffing Casserole: Substitute ⅓ cup cut-up cooked chicken for the turkey and ⅓ cup chicken gravy for the turkey gravy.

Corny Zucchini Combo

⅓ cup canned whole kernel corn, drained,
   from Old-fashioned Corn Relish
1 tablespoon hot water
¼ teaspoon instant chicken bouillon
   Dash each of dried rosemary leaves,
   crushed, and pepper
½ medium zucchini from Turkey Pot
   Roast, cut into ½-inch slices
1 teaspoon margarine or butter

Mix corn, water, instant bouillon, rosemary and pepper in ungreased 10-ounce casserole or custard cup. Top with zucchini; dot with margarine. Cover and cook in 350° oven until zucchini is tender, about 20 minutes.

Grapefruit Grenadine

Remove seeds from 1 chilled grapefruit half. Cut around edges and sections to loosen. Sprinkle with 1 to 2 teaspoons grenadine syrup.

1 Should Know...

Dried and instant forms are a boon for a single's staples shelf. When a recipe calls for fresh, but you're fresh out, you can rely on these substitutes:

1 clove garlic	= ¼ teaspoon instant minced garlic or ⅛ teaspoon garlic powder
¼ cup chopped onion	= 1 tablespoon instant minced onion or ½ teaspoon onion powder
1 tablespoon snipped parsley	= 1½ teaspoons dried parsley flakes
2 tablespoons chopped green pepper	= 1 tablespoon dried green pepper flakes
1 tablespoon snipped chives	= 1 teaspoon freeze-dried chives

TURKISH TURKEY
CHIVE-BUTTERED CARROTS
SALTY BREADSTICKS
CRANBERRY FREEZE

Turkish Turkey

¼ cup uncooked regular rice
2 tablespoons chopped onion
1 tablespoon chopped celery
1 tablespoon margarine or butter
½ cup water
⅓ cup cut-up cooked turkey from Turkey
    Pot Roast
2 tablespoons cut-up dried fruit
    (apricots, apples, pears and/or prunes)
1 teaspoon raisins
½ teaspoon instant chicken bouillon
⅛ teaspoon salt
    Dash each of ground cinnamon, dried
      thyme leaves and pepper
1 tablespoon chopped pecans

Cook and stir rice, onion and celery in margarine in 1-quart saucepan over medium heat until rice is light brown, about 6 minutes. Stir in remaining ingredients except pecans. Heat to boiling, stirring once or twice. Reduce heat; cover tightly and simmer 14 minutes. (Do not lift cover or stir.) Remove from heat. Fluff lightly with fork; cover and let steam 5 to 10 minutes. Sprinkle with pecans.

Chive-buttered Carrots

2 medium carrots
1 teaspoon margarine or butter
½ teaspoon frozen or freeze-dried chives
    Salt and pepper

Cut each carrot crosswise into halves. Cut each half lengthwise into ⅜-inch strips. Heat 1 inch salted water (½ teaspoon salt to 1 cup water) to boiling; add carrots. Cover; heat to boiling. Boil until tender, about 12 minutes; drain. Toss with margarine and chives. Sprinkle with salt and pepper.

Salty Breadsticks

Heat oven to 450°. Mix ¼ cup buttermilk baking mix and 1 tablespoon milk with fork until soft dough forms. Beat vigorously 30 seconds. Divide dough into halves; roll each half into stick, 6 inches long, with buttered hands. Place on ungreased cookie sheet or double thickness aluminum foil; sprinkle with salt. Bake until golden brown, 8 to 10 minutes.   2 breadsticks.

Cranberry Freeze

Mix ½ can (8-ounce size) whole cranberry sauce (about ½ cup) and ¼ cup sparkling water. Pour cranberry mixture into refrigerator tray; freeze until partially frozen, about 20 minutes. Turn into chilled large bowl or blender container. Beat until berries are broken and mixture is pink. Pour into refrigerator tray; freeze until firm, about 1 hour. Remove from freezer about 10 minutes before serving.

Cranberry Russian: Mix ½ cup Cranberry Freeze, softened, and 1 tablespoon vodka in tall glass. Fill glass with chilled sparkling water; stir. Garnish with orange or lemon slices if desired.

Index